CRAVING LONDON

CONFESSIONS OF AN INCURABLE ROMANTIC
WITH AN INSATIABLE APPETITE

JESSICA STONE

RIPE
PRESS

Ripe Press
1700 Sullivan Trail #134
Easton, PA 18040
United States of America

ISBN: 978-1-7351102-0-2
Ebook ISBN: 978-1-7351102-1-9

Jacket design and image by Andrea Warmington

Library of Congress Control Number: 2020911404

First paperback edition November 2020

www.jessicamstone.com

For my mother.

CONTENTS

PREFACE

I created fictional nicknames for the men in this book. This story is not about them, but about my journey. I believe that our external world mirrors what's inside us. The challenges I experienced with these people were borne out of whatever I needed to resolve for myself.

APPETIZER

("Starter," as they say over *there*.)

FORBIDDEN FRUIT

Summer 1998
The rectory of a Roman Catholic church in lower Manhattan

"HAVE you had sexual relations with him?" asked the young priest.

I looked away and squirmed. There was a large mahogany desk between us, making it feel more like I was at the principal's office rather than getting spiritual insight into the troubled relationship with my boyfriend.

"Well, it just happened for the first time last week," I admitted.

Now it was Father Michael who cast his gaze on nothing in particular. His office felt large, as if it could swallow me up. I noticed the small, bushy ponytail at the nape of his neck as I awaited his response, which seemed to take forever.

"You can be a virgin again," he cheerfully announced. "After confession."

The priest then leaned back in his large swivel chair, which looked like it belonged in a judge's chamber. He folded his hands under his chin, and said gravely, yet wistfully:

"But you've already tasted blood."

That may sound made up, but it's not. I have a thing for words, and a scarily good memory, perhaps owing to the fact that I'm slightly obsessive (OK, maybe more than "slightly"), and so I tend to replay conversations in my mind. Often. Besides, who can forget a line like that?

"You've already tasted blood."

I was 23 years old. The Boyfriend was all I knew—my first kiss, my first everything. I know, I came late to the game.

I'd met him a year before when I moved from Miami to get a master's degree in journalism at New York University. He was a software engineer from Los Angeles working at a tech startup in New Jersey. He had long blond hair, earrings, a tattoo, and he was a vegetarian—with little magnets on his fridge that read "No Pigs in Here" and "Cows Are Friends, Not Food."

There was no blood, anywhere.

He was the complete opposite of what anyone back home—including myself—thought I'd end up with. I'd grown up in a conservative Cuban family, surrounded by clean-cut guys who ate slabs of roasted pork and whole-milk rice pudding.

We were new territory to each other, in more ways than one. He introduced me to hummus and Trader Joe's; I taught him the difference between dancing salsa and merengue. Meanwhile, I'd explore the foreign contours of his body as if I were a scientist in a lab—sometimes giggling, always in wide-eyed wonder—while he waited patiently for me to get more and more comfortable with each breathless incremental increase in physical intimacy.

Seven years my senior, he found my innocence becoming. I'd let him inside my tiny graduate-student apartment only during the day. For whatever reason, I was worried I'd lose control at night. I was also concerned that my roommate would walk in on us. For our first few dates, we would only kiss—and kiss—on the street. Weeks later, when I finally let him in after the sun went down, I always kicked him out whenever things went too far for my comfort. He never protested.

"Want me to call you when I get home?"

"Nah, that's OK," I'd say, shooing him out the door.

Oh, to be that young and confident again.

Later, I found out he would sleep in his Ford Bronco so he didn't have to make the long drive home at 2 a.m.

This was love.

"I don't want my life to be a succession of men in my bed!" I wailed the first night I pondered letting him stay over.

He was lying on the twin mattress, the wall next to him scuffed by the leather bomber jacket and black jeans I made sure he kept on during our latest make-out session. Without missing a beat, he said:

"Then let your life be a succession of *me* in your bed."

With that kind of spontaneous poetry, how could I not let him stay? Suddenly, I went from wondering what was wrong with me because I'd never had a boyfriend to being with a guy who wanted to marry me. But we fought—a lot.

One night we were in a taxi heading to a Blur concert, and he was sulking because I had eaten a hamburger. When I asked him why he wouldn't let me make my own food choices, he thought about it and finally said, "Because it could affect those who come from you." He was referring to our future children. Even though I was angry, I had to laugh.

Those were the easy arguments. Others—about anything and everything—lasted well into the night before one of us realized we should just take off our clothes, because that was going to happen anyway.

"We may as well make up now" became a common refrain.

It was intense, exhilarating, and exhausting. I vacillated between wanting to run away and fearing I couldn't live without ever seeing The Boyfriend again. Meanwhile, his utter certainty that I was the woman for him both enthralled me and freaked me out. I wanted a man's undying devotion, but did it have to be the first guy I ever kissed?

He kept wanting to push our commitment forward, while I held back. So we would argue some more. Then he'd get mean, I'd start blaming, and we'd inevitably argue about how we were arguing. I lost track of how many times we'd break up only to get back together the next day.

And now here I was, sitting opposite a priest with a pony-tail, who didn't seem to care about the fact that I was falling apart and spending way too many hours arguing in traffic on the George Washington Bridge when I should have been savoring my new life in the city.

In my 40s I can see this so clearly, and at 23 I knew it some-where in my being, too. But I didn't trust myself, and I thought someone else would know more about what was better for me than I did. That's why I was sitting in front of Father Michael, hoping he would give me some kind of permission slip—a get-out-of-jail card I really could only give myself.

Instead, the priest was fixated on my recent "transgression."

"What about all the fighting?" I asked.

"That doesn't concern me as much; all marriages have trouble."

Trouble?

I didn't bother to correct the obvious—that I was young, that we weren't even engaged, and that perhaps we shouldn't even be together. But I was good at following orders—and ignoring my gut. So I dutifully went into the confession booth and made a vow to abstain. Then The Boyfriend visited the following weekend. Naturally, we ended up naked.

At brunch in the West Village the next day, I was distraught. I looked down at my eggs Florentine and cried, "I can't believe we did it again—I promised I wouldn't!"

"That's it, Babe, we're not doing it anymore," he said, slamming down his fork.

"Really?" I pouted.

We both laughed. But the mixture of desire and guilt consumed me.

Blame it on my Catholic education, although that didn't stop some of the other 10th-grade girls at La Salle High School from sneaking behind the bleachers with their boyfriends after pep rallies. Or the suggestive statues sprinkled throughout Florence—the Italian city that inspires gluttony and lust in equal measure while boasting an enormous concentration of churches.

I'd spent a month there studying Renaissance art right before The Boyfriend and I finally did the deed. It was the first time I understood that pleasures of the flesh and palate were deeply intertwined, and that food would become my sensual delight of choice when love wasn't around. I ate three gelatos a day while writing impassioned poetry to my man back home.

My preoccupation with romantic—and rather tragic—love started at an early age. Growing up in a Cuban family meant getting most of my love lessons from over-the-top Spanish-language soap operas—where lovers, consumed by fiery passion for each other, would let the rest of their lives melt into oblivion. As a child, I listened intently as my mother claimed she was instantly smitten with her first boyfriend, and noted the glint in my grandfather's eye when he recalled my grandmother flirting with him on a bus in 1940s Havana. They got off at the next stop and checked into a hotel. Scandalous. When she was seven months pregnant, they married. My grandparents spent four tumultuous years together before separating, during which time two more children—including my mother—were born. Then they obsessed about each other for the rest of their lives, even though they lived apart.

To me, the lesson was clear: Cupid's arrow was swift, sharp, and searing—leaving an indelible mark. At the same time, the nuns at St. Patrick School warned us about harboring lustful thoughts, which they said was just as sinful as carrying out the act. No wonder I was both terrified and captivated by *The Thorn Birds*, the epic tale of star-crossed love between a handsome priest and a much younger woman in the Australian outback. The popular television miniseries came out when I was only 8 years old, and I was riveted.

My father was a Russian Jew who was raised in Cuba, where he met my mother. They divorced when I was a baby, so my mother's Catholicism won out early on—much to the curiosity of my Jewish friends. One afternoon during summer camp in Miami Beach, I decided to teach them about the Immaculate Conception and the virgin birth of Jesus. Gathered in a circle with a rapt audience, it was my first experience as a storyteller. Too young to question what I had learned in school, I explained that Mary was born free from original sin and in turn had become pregnant with Jesus by the power of the Holy Spirit.

"That's the girl who told us about the Virgin Mary!" said one of my camp mates, pointing at me when her mother came to pick her up. The mother, gracefully, said nothing.

By the time I got to high school, I was going to Mass every day before class and had impressed the priests so much that they suggested I join the sisterhood.

"But I want to have kids," I told them.

And they could say nothing.

IMMACULATELY POACHED EGGS FLORENTINE
Makes one serving (multiply as you wish ...)

It took me forever to learn how to poach an egg. Poached eggs just seemed so advanced and risky to me—like losing one's virginity. But once you try making them, there's really not much to learn. And then you can have poached eggs all the time. Well, when you have a good egg.

For the Hollandaise:

2 egg yolks
1 tablespoon fresh lemon juice
Pinch cayenne
Pinch sea salt
½ stick (57 g) butter, melted

For the rest:

2 eggs
Handful of baby spinach
1 teaspoon butter
English muffin, split

First, make the Hollandaise:

1. Fill a small saucepan with ½ inch of water. Bring the water to simmer.
2. Place a stainless steel or glass bowl over the saucepan, making sure the bottom of the bowl doesn't touch the water.
3. Put egg yolks, lemon juice, cayenne, and salt into the bowl, then whisk together.

4. Add the melted butter in small increments, whisking well after each addition.

5. Continue whisking until thickened, then take off the heat and keep covered until ready to use.

For each egg (you can have two saucepans going at the same time):

1. Put a little white vinegar (about a tablespoon or two) into a small saucepan, then fill the pan with enough hot water to cover an egg (about two inches). Place over high heat.

2. Carefully crack the egg into a small ramekin.

3. When the water in the pan starts to boil, put a whisk into the water and rapidly whip it until you've created a whirlpool. Carefully tip the egg into the center of the whirlpool.

4. Lower the heat to barely simmering, and set the timer to four minutes. (I usually let it go about 15 seconds longer, because I like my egg yolk on the firmer side. Here, as with many things, personal preference will dictate how long you keep the egg in the pan.)

5. Use a slotted spoon to scoop up the egg, then gently shake off the excess water. You can also place the cooked eggs on a paper towel to soak up extra moisture.

Put it all together:

1. While the eggs are cooking, toast the English muffin halves. Melt the teaspoon of butter in a skillet, add the spinach, and cook—while stirring—until wilted.

2. Pile each muffin half with spinach, top with an egg, and spoon the Hollandaise on top.

BITTERSWEET SEPARATIONS

I was certainly not The Boyfriend's first, and I tortured both of us with questions about his romantic past. How, I wanted to know, could he be intimate with someone and then forget her? And how, specifically, could he be with me and not think about all of them? There was never a satisfactory answer, since it was impossible to grasp what I'd never experienced.

He bristled whenever I'd introduce him as "my first boyfriend," because to him it meant he would not be the last. So he tried to seal the deal. Several months after my confounding encounter with the priest, The Boyfriend proposed. As he got down on one knee, I instinctively tried to stop him. I actually bent down and tried to pull him up. Everything inside me was screaming no, and my body was trying to save me, but my brain decided that was simply not an appropriate response.

So I let go of my grip and said yes. And then I did nothing for a year. No bridal magazines, no moving in together, no planning of any sort. I was buying time. But for what?

When I finally gathered the courage to break off the engagement, the priest's advice became a premonition. Five years of celibacy ensued. Even if the relationship wasn't right, getting over my "first everything" turned out to be agonizing—everything in New York reminded me of him, and every guy I went on a date with just couldn't compare.

I consoled myself by eating my way around town and attempting to replicate my discoveries at home, including a drawn-out affair with the chocolate chip cookie at City Bakery.

The size of a bread-and-butter plate, the cookie's surface was cracked in all the right places to reveal a slightly lighter, softer interior, with the slightest, tiniest bubbles of molten butter breaking through. And of course, there was the chocolate. Deeply dark, it was more chunks than chips. The random pieces were sexy in their asymmetry.

In the buzz of the bakery, I created my own private rapture. After paying $2 at the counter, I would sit down and remove my cookie from its white sleeve, the paper already translucent from the butter. I'd carefully lift it up and inhale deeply for as long as I could stand it—about three seconds. It was the scent of a carefree childhood, of my chubby grandmother offering a sneaky taste before dinner.

Blinking slowly again, I'd let my teeth cut tenderly through the cookie. The ensuing tumble within me was rapid. I flipped the cookie upside down, so that now I tasted the cracked top. I kept turning it as I bit down, stopping every now and again to gaze in wonder at this new object of my affection.

I wanted to take it all in. I wanted to get under its sugary skin. I had to figure it out.

And so every weekend—usually Saturdays but sometimes Sundays if, heaven forbid, some pressure of regular life got in the way—I would go to the bakery, alone, for a rendezvous with my beloved. Lemony tarts, cheesecake-swirled brownies, and even double-chocolate cookies stared at me from the shelf, but I had an appetite only for my cookie.

Sometimes, while taking the express train there from my

studio in Brooklyn Heights, I would convince myself that I should try something new. But I just couldn't do it. Not to my taste buds. Not to my cookie.

As most smitten people do, I started talking about my cookie to my friends, then to colleagues and to out-of-town family. And, on more than one occasion, to complete strangers in bars. They'd look at me with polite amusement and slight concern while I heralded it as the best cookie in the universe. You can imagine my utter disbelief when I invited a friend to partake of my cookie worship by meeting me at City Bakery, only to discover she didn't think it was anything "that special." I was insulted, our friendship forever altered.

After a few weeks, I thought it might be worth a look around City Bakery. There was a refrigerated case displaying bake-at-home versions of the bakery's creations. With a mixture of skepticism and delight, I spotted a cute little sleeve of flecked dough marked "chocolate chip."

Was it possible that I could make my beloved cookie at home anytime I wanted? Could my cookie affair turn into a full-fledged romance?

I didn't even attempt to find out. The thought that my cookie could come out of a printed plastic sleeve like a sugar sausage was not a reality I was willing to live with. And why should I? I was aware of how powerfully the ritual of my habit had added to my singular devotion: the longing throughout the week, the excited awakening on Saturday mornings, the trek on the train, the hurried footsteps and mounting excitement on the way up to the bakery. I convinced myself that the vacuum-packed dough was an impostor, a pathetic substitute for THE ONE.

Only making the cookie from scratch at home would do, but I didn't think the chef would demystify his creation by parting with the recipe. So, on each visit, I continued to dissect the flavors in my mouth—lots of premium butter, granulated sugar, light brown sugar, vanilla extract (or was it the bean?), bitter-sweet Valrhona chocolate, stiffly beaten egg whites to get that cracked effect—and made a few wholehearted attempts in my truffle-sized kitchen. There were some pretty good results, but they weren't exactly right. Too flat. Not the right color. Something missing in the bite. Would I have to resign myself to a cookie on someone else's terms?

A baker's dozen or so cookie encounters had gone by when I hit upon the perfect plan. I would apprentice at the bakery. I would work—unpaid—in the kitchen, learning and watching my cookie emerge in all its seductive glory from the sum of its dusty, shiny, creamy parts.

Except I never asked for the job. And so the true inner workings of that cookie will forever remain a mystery to me: the whipped hows, the measured whys, the detailed whats.

Maybe that's exactly the way I liked it.

Because then I moved to London, where everything was a mystery.

APPETITE FOR ADVENTURE

New Year's Day 2004, the wee hours
The subway platform at 14th Street & Seventh Avenue in
Manhattan

WAITING ALONE for a train home to Brooklyn, I mused about the city that never sleeps. However great this place was, sleep was also good. And it was needed.

In a little over a week, I'd be on a plane to London—with no plans to use the return ticket. I felt as if I was reading the first chapter of a new book. I had no idea what was coming next in my life, and I was eager to turn the page.

By now, I'd lived in New York for seven years. After grad school and my breakup, I quickly learned that I couldn't afford to live in Manhattan on a reporter's salary while paying down my hefty student loans, so I sold my soul to the world of advertising. I was making a decent living as a copywriter, but before I turned 30 I also wanted to accomplish something else: living abroad. I wanted to challenge myself by dealing with uncertainty and throwing myself into a situation that required me to become a more flexible person. Nearing my 29th birthday with no husband and no kids, I concluded I had more to learn—and nothing to lose.

The "where" was easy. I'd been to the United Kingdom during my undergraduate years and was obsessed by the BBC adaptation of *Pride and Prejudice* starring Colin Firth as Mr. Darcy and Jennifer Ehle as Elizabeth Bennet. Darcy's inability to stop himself from falling madly in love with the self-assured Miss Bennet played right into all my romantic leanings.

London was an obvious choice.

My transatlantic move was, at times, a lonely slog. From concept to execution, it took a year and a half. I ate, breathed, and slept London—toiling night after night doing research, filling out paperwork, making connections. I applied for and got a visa—an arduous task that involved convincing the British government that I had marketable skills I'd put to good use on its soil. In exchange, I would be allowed the right to work. I just had to find someone to hire me. So I made two trips to London and met anyone who would talk to me over coffee or a pint.

Both times, I came back with a handful of new friends but no job. I soon realized I was not going to pull this off in the tidy way I had imagined. Unless I was there—on the ground—I wasn't going to get hired. I'd have to take a leap of faith. I'd need to fly into the unknown.

"Do it now before you own too much stuff, and your stuff owns you," my boss said when I told her the news. She had worked her way up to the top of the advertising ranks in New York City. Yet at my going-away party a few weeks later, she raised a glass to me and said, "Jessica's going to London, and she's going to marry a prince!"

I thought it was interesting that instead of focusing on my career, this self-made woman went straight to the romantic fairytale ending. And, I have to admit, I kind of liked it.

Another colleague looked downtrodden when I told him my plans.

"I feel like throwing my desk out the window," he said. "I wish I could do that; you're so brave."

"You can," I said. "The only difference between those who do and those who don't is just that—doing it."

Sometimes I could be so wise.

This move to London made me feel powerful. Despite my failure at moving on from my broken engagement, here was a project with definite steps and a goal that was materializing right before my eyes. I could make this happen, despite the naysayers—like the Australian creative director who said my experience in beauty advertising would never get me a job in England.

"It's not enough," he scoffed, telling me that British advertising was light years ahead.

I'd heard this before. British advertising was much more sophisticated and story-driven than on these shores, and beauty advertising in particular was considered fluff. There were also the differences between American and British English, which went far beyond spelling. I'd have to learn an entirely new culture in order to communicate and sell.

The odds were seemingly against me. But the idea of starting over—unencumbered—thrilled me. That's when I discovered the power of fear as a signpost. It means "keep going."

And there was something else. I'd heard that London had a much higher ratio of men to women than the Big Apple. I'd been unattached for four years by now, and I hoped that a change of scenery would also usher in a new love—one that would finally rip the old one from my heart.

So before I left, I said goodbye. I went to the courtyard near Washington Square Village—just inside the graduate-housing complex I lived in, right under my old apartment. That same courtyard The Boyfriend and I used to sit in for hours and just kiss, and where I'd worry my roommate would see us.

I sat there alone, in the same place—on the same bench, under the same tree. I could almost feel The Boyfriend's fingers crawling up the back of my neck while he whispered, "You just wait, I can really make you tingle."

But this time, instead of welling up with tears at the memory, I smiled.

I was ready.

POUND FOR POUND

I DID IT.

I quit my job, got rid of my Brooklyn studio along with all the IKEA furniture in it, and prepared to take flight—with $10,000 in savings to my name.

My move depended as much on the kindness of strangers as it did on handling all the administrative business that comes with making something like this happen without a cushy expat package. Even though I had no job and no promise of anything, my two trips had paid off—I had amassed a solid network in London. By the time I was ready to go, I had someone to pick me up at Heathrow at six in the morning, a place to crash for the first few weeks, and lots of "mates" to meet at the pub.

This wasn't a wait-and-see endeavor. I didn't give myself the option of a plan B. My plan A, B, C, all the way through Z, was "make this work."

I didn't realize it at the time, but I was essentially living the law of attraction. My thoughts were oriented only in the direction of London, thus creating my new reality.

I had scheduled no fewer than 30 interviews for the first 20 days. Carrying the famous A to Z (pronounced "zed") map book of London streets, I pounded the agency-rich Soho area while juggling my portfolio and an umbrella that was forever twisting itself inside out in the slushy mix of January sleet, rain, and snow.

The look: a black crepe blazer paired with a variety of trousers from the days I wrote catalog copy for J.Crew. London being a much larger city than New York with no time for pit stops, whatever I wore in the morning had to last me well into the evening.

With neither time nor money to waste, I was all about strategy. I quickly discovered where I could go to the bathroom on Oxford Street without having to spring for a cup of coffee. In between, I'd pore over *Advertising Age* magazine, highlighter in hand, noting the creative execs who were leaving one agency and moving to another. This signaled to me a reshuffling of priorities and the need for fresh blood, which meant a potential opening for me.

Some people were impressed—they saw my solo move as a character asset. During one interview, I felt like I was on the evening news:

"So, Jessica, this is a massive leap you've taken. Tell me, what drives you, what keeps you going?"

Other days wouldn't go so well. Around interview number 25, I was told to burn my portfolio, go back to college, and make no further appointments—and in a very polite English accent, which made it even worse. This was emotional boot camp. My skin grew thicker, and I became convinced that advertising was an evil, pompous clique.

Meanwhile, my bank account and my waistline were rapidly dwindling. The British pound was at an all-time high, at 1.82 to the US dollar. I was converting everything to dollars in my head and would balk in horror at supermarket-brand orange juice costing nearly $7.

I would have to start making concessions. Here was my brilliant plan: I would eat the cheapest sandwich at Pret A Manger —the egg and cress—every day for lunch, day after day. By night, it was cheese tortellini with tomato basil sauce from Sainsbury's, the local supermarket. Years later, I realized that my routines were actually a very effective productivity technique. My minimalist approach wouldn't just save me money; it saved me valuable thinking time. In between, I was putting in eight-hour days at Caffè Nero, looking for jobs online and snacking on sea salt and cracked black pepper crisps.

Despite the challenges, these were early days in my love affair with my new country, and I was enamored of everything British. Exhausted every night when I climbed into bed, visions of BBC adaptations still danced in my head. One Saturday night while shopping for my predictable tortellini after a whole day at Nero, I happened to spot him in one of the aisles— wearing a black peacoat, jeans, and a little black-and-red beanie. I gasped. Colin Firth! Alone! In *my* Sainsbury's! It was like seeing an ex-boyfriend. I recognized him right away, and my heart stopped. Then it started beating very fast. *Mr. Darcy* was at the market, pushing a trolley (the British have a way of making even shopping carts sound quaint). I followed him around for a while, too starstruck to get close enough and peek at his selection of groceries. I swear he kept looking at me too, probably thinking, "Oh no, another dodgy one."

I was not exactly my best self. Drained from back-to-back meetings where I'd hear lots of praise but no firm offers, I started feeling like a big fraud and losing the power to tell myself, "Chin up, chin up." It was no wonder the weight was falling off. Within three weeks, I had dropped eight pounds.

NO STRESS EGG AND CRESS
Makes one on-the-run sandwich

The key to egg salad—aside from properly cooked eggs—is to chop them well. I use a pastry blender. Oh, and go easy on the mayo. You need less than you think.

2 eggs
1 tablespoon good mayonnaise
¼ teaspoon Dijon mustard
½ celery stalk, thinly sliced
Dash sea salt
Freshly ground pepper
Sprig of watercress, washed and torn
Two slices of whole-grain or rye bread

1. Place eggs in a saucepan, cover with cold water, and add a dash of salt. Set pan over high heat.
2. As soon as the water starts to boil, cover the pan, turn off the heat, and set the timer for 11 minutes. Meanwhile, fill a bowl with water and ice.
3. When the timer goes off, transfer eggs to the bowl.
4. Peel the cooled eggs.
5. Put eggs, mayonnaise, mustard, and celery into a bowl. Mash it all up until the eggs are finely chopped and everything is mixed together. If you don't have a pastry blender (although you really should get one), use a fork and knife to chop and mix. Season with salt and pepper to taste.
6. Sandwich the egg salad and watercress between the bread slices. Eat and get back to your to-do list.

FIRST COURSE

EATING IS CHEATING

"YOU LOOK LIKE AN INSECT!" gasped Charlie, my very first London friend.

I had met Charlie in New York's Central Park through a mutual acquaintance while I was thinking about the big move. Now here we were, catching up over drinks in Leicester Square —London's version of Times Square.

Charlie was nearing 32 and seriously afraid she'd be "left on the shelf" if she didn't meet someone soon, so she had ramped up her search for a man in the feverish yet methodical way I was approaching my job hunt. She begged me to go to a speed dating event with her, and I reluctantly agreed. I really had other things on my mind. Even though I had been single for years, starting over in London made me feel absolved of my past. It also gave me the confidence that I could make anything happen, and that I had plenty of time for love.

"You'll have no problem here—you American girls are so perfectly groomed all the time! But you need to gain some weight."

She was right—I was disappearing beneath my clothes. It

wouldn't last long. Only four weeks after I arrived at Heathrow —weary and excited and pushing five suitcases—I scored my first freelance gig. I'd be writing recruitment ads for TK Maxx, the UK version of TJ Maxx. With steady money coming in, an increased caloric intake would follow.

Now the question was where to live. I didn't want to get sucked into the familiar allure of the American expat community. I wanted to immerse myself in the British way of life. And because I didn't know how much money would be coming in month to month, I decided I'd better get a "flatmate"—an English one. Her name was Rosie, she came from a conservative Christian family in Birmingham, and, miraculously, she let me move in without a security deposit.

The flat was in Chiswick, a very charming area of west London with the nicest "high street" I'd ever seen. Like any high street, Chiswick High Road had everything one could possibly need: Sainsbury's, Caffè Nero, Boots (pharmacy), WH Smith (stationers), Waterstones (books), Marks & Spencer (everything for you, your home, and your appetite), along with health-food stores, all manner of restaurants, cute clothing shops, and, of course, pubs. It's an affluent suburb, home to celebrities and young families pushing expensive prams around the pretty, leafy neighborhood.

Immediately, Rosie got to work introducing me to important British cultural institutions. One of the most interesting and disturbing of these was the cauliflower ear. Now most of you living beyond British shores might think I stumbled upon a petite variety of the dimpled vegetable, but no. The ear in question is a real one, one that can be spotted on rugby players, particularly those who find themselves smashing their skulls together in what is affectionately called "the scrum." Short for "scrummage," it's a bizarre, beastly huddle designed to regain possession of the ball. Cauliflower ears result from trauma as a result of the scrum—internal bleeding leads to blood clots appearing on the visible part of the ear.

Rosie was a hardcore rugby fan and devotee of *Top Gear*, a show on the "telly" about cars. She should have been every man's dream, so it was refreshing—and utterly comforting—to live with her and her boy troubles. I also received an altogether unexpected lesson: how dating dilemmas cross cultures. She and her friends were plagued by the same struggles as their American counterparts when it came to finding love—with the exception that they were more adept at texting than we were. When I arrived in London in the winter of 2004, texting was still relatively new in the US.

Rosie tried to explain rugby to me at least half a dozen times and even took me to a match so I could experience the "magic" firsthand. But alas, the only thing that stuck was the cauliflower ear, especially when I caught a glimpse of an actual specimen, bulbous and distorted, on the Underground. The memory still haunts me.

The other notable difference between Rosie's single life and mine was the amount of drinking involved. The supermarket was a 10-minute walk away—including a bridge and tunnel—but three pubs were always within crawling distance.

Brits love alcohol and food in equal measure, but they rarely come together on a "big night" unless by accident. A big night refers to one in which there is no change of clothing in a 24-hour period and the boss comes to work the next day at noon proudly announcing her hangover. I could see why. Food was more of an afterthought, as in, "Let's pop into the kebab place on the way home," or, "I'll just grab a bag of crisps (potato chips) with the next round."

The aim of the game is to get drunk as quickly as possible. The reasoning goes like this:

Food gets in the way. Dinner slows down the intoxication

process. It takes time to find a restaurant and get a table. Why do that when you can just claim a bar stool for the night until you fall off it, completely "shattered"? In their words, eating is cheating.

Some said this was a throwback to the days when pubs would close early, leading to drinking straight through dinner. Others argued that the once-bemoaned British cuisine was not exactly an incentive for breaking away from the booze. Either way, I was entirely unprepared for it. On my first—and last—big night, I inadvertently consumed an entire bottle of red wine while being too polite to ask when we'd be going to dinner. These were after-work drinks with my new colleagues at The Body Shop, where I was writing copy about the same toiletries I coveted when I was in college. It was a much more lucrative long-term freelance assignment, and I wanted to give the impression that I fit in.

I tried to drink with the best of them, but when I stumbled to the "loo" and looked in the mirror, I saw that I had aged about 15 years. My mouth was stained with merlot, as if I had clumsily smeared a gigantic lipstick around it. Only later did I learn what my work mates had been up to: they wanted to "baptise the American girl."

When I returned to the group, I decided to lay my head on the art director's lap for a little nap.

"Should I take you home?" he inquired.

I thanked him and said no. I still had the wits to worry that he was only trying to get into my pants. To his credit, he asked me to tell him exactly how I was getting home—twice—in order to make sure I could.

"The Jubilee Line to Green Park to the Piccadilly Line to Turnham Green to the 94 Bus," I slurred, and managed to repeat it.

How I got back to the flat all the way from London Bridge, I still don't know. But I wasn't able to lift my head the next morning. Shattered, indeed.

THE QUEEN'S HEAD ENGLISH

THE COLORFUL PUB names in the UK are as plentiful as the establishments themselves. Often some variation of "The Queen's Head" or a joyful combination such as "Slug and Lettuce," it behooves you to learn the names, along with some other handy expressions.

Proper: Very useful, except when it's not. Ponder this tagline for Byron, a UK restaurant chain: "Proper Hamburgers." Tell me, what is an improper burger?

Set off: Head off, get going, go. As in, "When do you plan to set off?" Receives perplexed looks stateside.

G.P.: General Practitioner, or primary-care physician, with whom you need to register through the beloved National Health Service (NHS). Note for the ladies: Don't freak out when the nurse giving you your Pap smear is called "sister." It's a remnant of the religious origins of nursing.

Would do, could do, should do: Very odd-sounding to American ears. Frequently used in response to questions. Such as, "You really should have a proper meal after all those pints you had last night." Answer: "Yes, I should do."

Whereabouts: Great one. "Whereabouts in the city can I get proper fish and chips?"

Curry: Insanely delicious and greasy Indian food. "After all those pints we just had, why don't we go for a curry?" Note the use of "a" before "curry" designating this is a big deal.

Knackered: "I can barely keep my eyes open; I'm knackered."

Sort: Figure it out. "I'll leave it to you peeps to sort out." Also used in place of "fix." "I need to sort my lunch."

A half: Half pint. Pronounced "hawlf." "What, you're only going to have half a cider? Come on, this round's on me."

Fit: Hot. "Ewan McGregor is really fit!" Don't you agree?

Hire: Rent. You hire a car in the UK, which made me a little nervous at first, thinking I was going to have to shell out for a chauffeur.

Fancy: Somewhere between like and lust lies fancy. "Yes, he acted like a complete twat, but I still fancy the pants off him." (More on this later.)

Bits: Parts of your body. This one really got me at first, and it still makes me cringe. You'll often see it in sun cream (read: sunscreen) ads: "Cover up your most delicate bits." Hmm.

Taking the piss/taking the mickey: Making fun. "He was just taking the piss when he said he was going teetotal tonight." Side note: Taking the piss is considered a high compliment in Britain. It means you're "in." As one native told me: "The British make fun of you to your face; Americans do it behind your back."

Night bus: What you're taking to get home after the Tube stops running. Also erroneously referred to as the "fright bus." Everybody takes it, and it's nowhere near as scary as the price of a cab.

The Knowledge: The incredible amount of information you must know to be a cabbie—much more than just street smarts. Always talk to your cabbie.

Fortnight: Simply, two weeks. But sounds regal and romantic.

Cheeky: Extremely useful and polite expression when referring to someone who is being either a little too clever or out of line. "Russell Brand is such a cheeky

&%^!"

XXX: Not what you think. Sign-off for texts and emails equivalent to the American xoxo. The number of Xs is of supreme importance. "Uh-oh, he only put one X at the end of his text. Whatever do you think it means?"

PRE-PUB CRAWL CAULIFLOWER CURRY
Makes two generous, stomach-lining servings

There is one thing I definitely got in Britain: Indian food. Most curry joints are actually Bangladeshi or Pakistani. Either way, all of them will feature cauliflower in at least several incarnations. This easy recipe always manages to wow company. Feel free to substitute seasonal vegetables for the green peas. Sweet potato and spinach work very well here.

    4 tablespoons coconut oil
    1 onion, chopped
    3-4 cloves garlic, chopped
    1 tablespoon root ginger, minced
    2 teaspoons mild korma powder (mild curry powder)
    75 g (about 2.6 ounces) red lentils
    400 ml (about 13.5 ounces) vegetable stock (I use
    Marigold Vegan Bouillon)
    2 tablespoons vegetarian curry paste
    1 cauliflower, cut into small florets
    200 ml (½ can) coconut milk
    1 cup (150 g) green peas
    2 tablespoons chopped fresh cilantro/coriander
    Juice of half a lemon

1. Melt half of the oil in a saucepan over medium heat.
2. Add the onion, garlic, ginger, and korma powder and fry for about five minutes.
3. Add the lentils, stir well, and pour in the stock. Bring to the boil. Cover and lower the heat to simmer for 25 minutes (lentils should be tender).
4. Meanwhile, heat the remaining oil in a fry pan. Add the curry paste and fry gently for 3 minutes.
5. Add the cauliflower and stir-fry another 3 minutes. Remove from the heat.
6. Add the coconut milk and cauliflower to the lentils and return to the boil. Cover and simmer for 10 minutes.
7. Stir in the green peas, cilantro/coriander, and lemon juice.
8. Heat through for 3 minutes and serve over brown basmati rice (I got hooked on Tilda brand.)

BANANA PANCAKES AND THE
(UN)DATING GAME

THE SPEED-DATING event was already swarming with singles when Charlie and I arrived. Speed dating was a relatively new concept here, yet it looked like people were hungry for it.

Charlie was compulsively touching up her lip gloss. Justin Timberlake's "Rock Your Body" was playing through the speakers. A woman with a giant camera swooped in on me paparazzi style, so I "agreed" to pose for the wall of "Lonely Hearts." The idea was to browse the pictures for any potential candidates who caught your eye and leave a sticker with your nickname on it. Mine was Cookie Monster, for obvious reasons. But before I could check out the men's section, we were rushed in for the speed-dating portion of the event.

First up was City Boy. "The City" refers to the Square Mile —the area of central London that is home to major financial institutions. I'd heard about the men who worked there and their pinstripe suits. And here was one of them, a gregarious trader sipping a cocktail held gingerly between perfectly mani-cured fingers—right down to the clear nail polish. But this didn't bother me as much as what came next.

Apparently nervous (or not), City Boy launched into an ode

to his former (male) flatmate, whom he wished his next girl-friend would emulate. He said they bonded when they both broke up with their girlfriends at the same time and needed a place to share. They got along well—exceptionally well. At one point, one of the beds broke. So he and the flatmate did the most logical thing: they slept together.

City Boy recounted the experience:

"He had this annoying habit of letting his alarm clock ring on and on. So one day I got pissed, climbed over him, and my willy nearly went in his mouth. That shut him up."

And with that, our three minutes were up.

There it was. My first taste of London dating—or, as I was to learn, (un)dating.

I didn't know if the guy was making up the story and "taking the piss," but I didn't have the stomach to keep going. When I looked over at Charlie, I saw that her bubbly mood had consid-erably darkened and she was clearly trying to get away from the current man in her speed-dating queue. On the bus home, she confessed to me that she was really there to get her mind off a younger guy she had "pulled" (hooked up with) at a party the week before. They had wound up in bed, and she panicked when his parting words the next morning were simply, "See you around."

I found dating in London to be impossible, mostly because it didn't exist, at least not in the American sense. Gwyneth Paltrow (pre-Chris Martin) once famously lamented the lack of dating in England, so you know the situation is dire. The reason it didn't exist is that dating was considered an American concept that amounted to hedging one's bets. The British looked upon our courtship customs with a mixture of skepticism and morbid curiosity. There was even an article about it in one of the freebie newspapers handed out in the Tube: "US-Style Multi-Dating Sweeps UK!"

In London, it seemed the norm to cut out the dating part and jump straight into a full-fledged relationship. Charlie was a case in point. Her guy kept his word, and they quickly became exclusive.

The practice of going to the pub with your colleagues made things even trickier—you never quite knew who was available. There was the information architect with the devilish stare (an entirely accurate description), the Cockney guy who pinched my butt (they're allowed to do that at work?!), and the Australian illustrator who kept showing me his sketches (does he even realize what he's doing?) None of them actually made a move, and I'd entertain *Portrait of a Lady* fantasies where I was desired by all three of them.

Not wanting to take a risk, I got cozy with a much more dependable discovery: sticky toffee pudding.

Sticky, toffee, pudding: three words I'd come to cherish on a menu. It's not pudding in the typical sense. The British sometimes refer to dessert as pudding, something that confused and bothered me until I got over it and got hot and bothered by the spiced, dense, sickly-sweet combination of dates, dark brown sugar, and drizzly warm caramel sauce.

The only other cake I'd craved like this came in the form of Magnolia Cupcakes in New York. I had consumed so many of them that I can still taste the buttercream icing on my tongue if I close my eyes. I had not been able to court another cupcake since. Likewise, I became faithful to the sticky toffee pudding at The Abingdon in Kensington, the part of town Americans seemed to gravitate toward and that I avoided specifically for that reason—until I discovered this particular rendition of sticky toffee pudding. I'd ask for it with vanilla ice cream instead of the typical clotted cream. The restaurant staff didn't seem to mind, or at least they pretended not to.

I didn't expect to fall in love with the food in my adoptive country, and not just because I foolishly believed the rumors about unappetizing British cuisine. I had learned to eat in New York, and I was not going to let something else take its place. I resisted at first: coming to grips with trading bagels for scones; Monterey Jack for Somerset Cheddar; Fairway and Zabars for Fresh & Wild. After my initial hard-headedness, I started surrendering to this new contender and the quirks that eventually won me over.

Meanwhile, I was getting used to my new life and developing some routines. As a single girl in New York, I had lots of little "me" rituals. Every Saturday, I'd treat myself to pancakes at the now-defunct Veg City Diner on 14th Street near Sixth Avenue.

Because diners are as nonexistent as dating in London, I came up with another solution. Faithfully, weekend in and weekend out, I made up these fluffy little numbers and drenched them with real Vermont syrup that cost about £40. I swore I was singlehandedly keeping North American maple farmers in business.

The recipe might seem time-consuming at first, but after a couple of weekends, you'll be making it with your eyes closed. It makes a perfect stack for one but is easily doubled. So, should you find yourself in the happy situation of waking up with someone deserving of banana pancakes, you know what to do.

BANANA PANCAKES WITH
BLUEBERRY THRILL COMPOTE
Makes one generous stack

For the pancakes:

¼ cup (34 g) all-purpose flour (plain flour in the UK)

¼ cup (34 g) spelt flour

Dash sea salt

One handful well-chopped walnuts (about ¼ cup)

1 tablespoon ground flax seeds

Pinch ground cinnamon

½ teaspoon baking powder

¼ teaspoon baking soda

1 egg

2 tablespoons plain Greek yogurt (not low-fat!)

About ½ cup (118 ml) water

1 ½ tablespoons butter

1 ripe banana

For the compote:

½ cup (80 g) frozen blueberries

1 tablespoon maple syrup

½ teaspoon cornstarch (called corn flour in the UK)

1. First, make the pancakes. Mix all the dry ingredients together with a fork.
2. In a separate bowl, beat the egg, then whisk in the yogurt and the water.
3. Stir the wet ingredients into the dry, adding more water, if needed, to make a thick batter that will still pour easily.
4. Heat a heavy nonstick skillet over medium heat. Add a ½ tablespoon of butter and tilt the pan around so the butter swirls and coats the bottom.
5. Pour in some batter to make pancake-sized circles, and cook until bubbles start to form on top.
6. Flip and cook the other side. Repeat two more

times, transferring each pancake to a plate lined with paper towel to keep them from getting soggy.

7. Slice the banana diagonally into thin slices and set aside.

8. Meanwhile, combine the blueberries, maple syrup, and cornstarch in a small saucepan, and set over medium heat.

9. Stir constantly until compote thickens, using a potato masher to release the juice from the berries.

10. Layer the bananas between the pancakes, spoon on the blueberry compote, and wonder how on earth you happen to be single.

SINGLE AND HUNGRY

MY WEEKENDS in London were anchored by two rituals: banana pancakes on Saturday and the newspaper on Sunday. The Sunday paper must be read almost in its entirety, beginning with the magazine—to get it out of the way—then the monthly supplement before moving on to the paper itself, which undoubtedly ends with a painful skimming of the real estate section. Reading these property listings is like walking into Harvey Nichols (the posh department store in Knightsbridge) after you've paid the rent—why bother when you can't buy?

The upside of being single is that your weekend rituals can happen whenever you please. Being single also means you can subsist entirely on snacks, usually in combinations to which you'd never subject anyone else. A bowl of applesauce and yogurt with a side of popcorn for dinner? Been there, eaten that.

Yet another "bonus" of singledom is being able to sample from a wide range of pastimes. As such, I began taking Ceroc lessons. Billed as a fusion of salsa and jive, Ceroc involves rotating dance partners so that by the end of the night you've touched every sweaty palm in the place.

Every Monday night, I headed up to North London for the

three-hour affair. First, there was the 45-minute beginners' class. Claire, the highly spirited instructor with masses of redheaded (which the English call "ginger") curls, would introduce her partner as "the demo." Together, they demonstrated the moves for the night, culminating in a whiplash routine.

Someone has had a lot of fun coming up with the names for these steps. There's the Octopus: "Guys, wrap the ladies; ladies, wrap the man; men, wrap the ladies," or the slightly too-close-for-comfort Comb: "Guys, return the lady, drape her free hand over your neck, and wiggle, wiggle for a count of one ... two."

After a brief freestyle session, the intermediate class began. It involved double turns and lots of fancy footwork. One week, we learned the Back Bend: "Now ladies, if you have a bad back (i.e. if you don't want your pelvis anywhere near your partner), you don't have to do it."

Throughout, we were told that we needed to let the man lead. Even if he has no idea what he's doing, we still need to let him think he does. We should understand that his job is harder, as he actually has to *think* about his next move. And if he can command the lead, the dance will flow seamlessly. Hmm, sound familiar?

After three hours of push-spinning, tumble drying, basket weaving, and wiggle-wiggling, there was only one thing to do: go home and open the fridge. And when you need a quickie, nothing beats a good old peanut butter and jam sandwich. My favorite calls for lots of texture in each element so that this, the simplest rendition of the Earl of Sandwich's invention, rises to a higher, grander sweet-and-salty level.

One night, my dance partner leaned in to whisper what I thought would be a sweet compliment about my moves.

"You need to let the man lead," he said, the spreading sweat on his shirt suddenly jumping out at me.

His stern, paternal tone ran straight down my spine as he spun me sharply.

I never went back to class.

LEAD ME OR LEAVE ME
PEANUT BUTTER AND JAM
Makes a solo sandwich

The bread: sourdough rye from the Old Post Office Bakery in South London. Toasted. The PB: Biona Organic, crunchy. Always crunchy. The jam: Bonne Maman wild blueberry. The result: a seamlessly perfect pas de deux if I ever did taste one.

PLAYING WITH FIRE

AFTER A YEAR of freelancing and making more money than I ever did back in New York, I landed a steady job at an ad agency and moved into my own place in Brook Green—a quiet pocket in Hammersmith, also in west London.

Everything had fallen into place deliciously. All the gut busting and pavement pounding had paid off; I was now settled in as a Londoner. It was the first of many lessons. Had I made the move with a job offer and expat package in the conventional way, I would have been shackled with "golden handcuffs"—and my life in London would have depended on something outside of me. Having a company handle my relocation might have been easy, but it would have stripped me of autonomy and fulfillment. Instead, I had done it myself, on my terms. It's only when I wasn't afraid to lose it all that I stood the most to gain. And with that, I discovered the resourcefulness I could always count on within myself.

It was time for a celebration—and a new challenge. My pick: culinary school. I had dreamed about it forever, and the London branch of Le Cordon Bleu was just a few blocks away from the ad agency. I could not afford to quit my job and dedicate myself to a full-time program, so I decided on an intensive course in basic patisserie. I told my boss that she could either keep me on part time, or I was leaving and going freelance. She wanted me to stay—on the condition that I'd bring samples from class. Deal.

It had been over seven years since I had been a student. This time, I was carrying a case of Wüsthof knives and going to class in Marylebone—not Greenwich—Village. Madonna lived there, surrounded by some of the best food shops in London.

The course ran twice a week with a demonstration in the morning and a practical class in the afternoon, where I and nine other students—wearing traditional white double-breasted jackets—tried to re-create the day's recipe. The other three days, I was at the agency.

We spent the first week perfecting a puff pastry filled with poached pears and almond cream. I won't even attempt to transcribe the procedure, because no sane person would ever make it at home. As I sat there, I doubted I ever would. This was exhausting work. With mixing and rolling and chilling the pastry (several times), preparing and poaching the pears, making the crème, piping it onto the pastry, layering the pears over, making a lattice crust, baking it, glazing it, and plating it, the entire process took Chef Philippe 2 ½ hours. It gave me a newfound admiration for the profession, and I'm now convinced that $5 for a croissant is a total steal.

The demo room had a mirror above the chef so we could see exactly what he was doing, even if you're petite like me. I filled six full-size pages—both sides—with notes. The scent of pears simmering in vanilla, cinnamon, and rum climbed to dizzying heights, teasing the hunger already churning beneath the high waist of my checkered trousers.

Finally, the goods came out of the oven. This was the moment I had been waiting for. I picked up the warm slice and bit through it in slow motion, falling into a trance. The room disappeared, and I was suddenly in the autumnal countryside, where London's traffic noise had been replaced with the sound of a leaf pile swirling in the wind. The hot, squishy pear flecked with vanilla beans pooled and then dissolved in my mouth, followed by a creamy slip of sugared almonds that demanded a meditative bite. The toasted, paper-thin flakes from the pastry floated onto my jacket. I was completely lost to the moment.

"Don't forget to bring your scales and hats to the practical," said Chef Philippe, rousing me from my reverie.

Back at the office, I was grappling with one distinct feature of London advertising agencies: the open bar.

On the ground floor, immediately to your left after pushing through the glass doors, the bar came alive every Tuesday night. It used to be every night—until the cleaners refused to do their work because the mess had gotten so out of hand.

It boggled my mind that we had no air conditioning in the building, yet drinks were free. I was also peeved, because this employee "perk" was completely lost on me. Free cake, I'll take. But an open bar? No point when I could nurse a glass of wine for hours.

The bar was the place to get cozy with your colleagues under the guise of inebriation, and bosses were typically absent. My boss was a tall, slender blonde who had relocated from San Francisco. She was in her late 40s and taught me random yet entirely useful tidbits, such as why it was important to apply moisturizer to one's décolletage—and to start in your 30s. She warned that the skin there was especially fragile and prone to wrinkling, which was visible upon awakening if you sleep curled up on your side. I've been moisturizing my chest ever since.

She also taught me a neat trick for quickly freshening up the pasta she would sometimes pack for her lunch: with a spray of rocket (arugula) she brought in a separate container.

Then there was the simple productivity tip I've used since she first shared it with me: make sure to touch anything only once. Whether you're going through bills or sorting laundry, handle each and every item one time only. If you're going to open an email, answer it right then and there.

The boss had also hoped to find her English gentleman, yet despite her career accomplishments and treasure trove of handy life advice, she was coming up empty when it came to dating.

Inevitably, our morning status meetings became morning-after debriefs.

"He's an Oxford grad, has his own business, was a perfect gentleman, and he even texted me on the way home," the boss said.

"But?" asked the art director.

The boss slouched in her chair and sighed.

"No jump factor," I said.

They all got what I meant, but they wanted to know more. I came up with the term "jump factor" to describe that elusive quality that makes you want to jump someone's bones. It's normally indirectly correlated to how great they look on paper. A vexing experience, for sure. Even more frustration—and certainly damage—comes from wanting to jump people who are entirely inappropriate for you and will only cause you pain. These include "the one-sided jump," and the urge to jump those who are much too good-looking for your own good—such as The Barrister.

In the UK, a barrister is a lawyer who provides specialist legal advice and can plead a case before the High Court.

I first laid eyes on The Barrister during a networking event organized by my friend Margaret, a business journalist. The

Barrister looked like a young Robert De Niro, he was smart and sarcastic, and he paid almost no attention to me at all. I was immediately intrigued.

When Margaret invited me to a dinner party, I secretly hoped he'd be there. Margaret is a gifted cook with a knack for bringing together wonderfully different personalities, making for sparkling conversation.

There were eight of us. To my right, a professor—impeccably dressed and with that English boyishness that made Hugh Grant so lovable. To my left, a wine writer—California transplant, blushed easily. Across from me, Margaret, and next to her, The Barrister, who was trying to lay off the alcohol.

"I promised myself I won't touch the wine tonight," The Barrister announced upon seeing the row of glasses before him.

Next to him was a pop-culture maven, also American. Most downloaded and banned episode of *South Park*? She knew it. And could quote from it, too. At the other end of the table was a fashion stylist, recently on a job with Victoria Beckham (confirmed: size 2 jeans). Coming full circle, we had Margaret's mother, one of the most well-traveled and insightful women I'd ever met.

The conversation was electric and covered the most enticing dinner-party topics: politics (then-Secretary of State Condoleezza Rice's 4 a.m. workout routine), sex (the guys in *Brokeback Mountain* were shepherds, not cowboys, dammit!), and religion ("Sunday Roast" does not necessarily follow church).

After numerous courses, the *tarte au citron* I had made in class arrived at the table. A crust of pâte brisée—made by rubbing butter and flour between the fingers until it feels like sand—cradles a tangy lemon curd and is crowned with snow-white meringue piped like stars, edges burnished with a blowtorch.

Spoons dip through for the first bite. The professor starts to plot ways to marry me off. The fashion stylist coos approvingly.

"It's ... correct," proclaims the wine writer.

I catch The Barrister eyeing his spoonful inquisitively. He swallows, and in his baritone declares: "This says don't eat me, shag me."

Margaret let out a hearty laugh, and the rest of us followed suit. In that moment, we were his court—captive and unanimously convinced.

As I walked home alone that night, I began to suspect that everyone around the table had a thing for The Barrister. Cambridge-educated and athletic, he seemed to be the most eligible bachelor in our circle of friends. And he knew it. The fact that he could tell I "fancied" him was as clear as the smirk above the half-empty wine glass he said he wouldn't touch.

"How did our lives wind up this way?"

These were the words my boss scribbled down and slipped to me in the middle of what felt like an endless status meeting.

We were in a standard "pre-pro"—a pre-production call before you shoot a TV commercial. It's where you go from a "quick 'n rough"— a low-budget mock-up of the ad—to a "full up." And it's a staggeringly expensive endeavor, even if you're just selling tubes of mascara, which is what we were doing. Everyone on the team—creatives (i.e. copywriters like me and our art-director counterparts), brand managers, production people, director, casting agent, and the too-many-to-count VPs—gathered around a spaceship-like receiver in the middle of a mammoth boardroom table, with the client on the other end of the line.

This was the world of beauty advertising, and it was ugly.

Very ugly. This is where you hear things like, "But nostrils have never been a problem before!" after a client complains that a model tilted her head just a millimeter too high. This is where highly-paid executive VPs sigh, "I'm losing the will to live," before ordering lunch from Nobu. This is also where that same model with (heaven forbid) nostrils stops by the catering spread on a shoot, drags her finger along the inside of a cake pan, and allows herself the smallest stolen pleasure of buttery crumbs—the waistband of her Blue Cult jeans hovering like a hula hoop over her jutting hip bones.

Despite my fondness for all those free lunches, they came with too high a price. I knew I had to get out. My decision to go part-time and jump into culinary training had already set me on a path elsewhere, and that note my boss handed to me was all I needed to know. I did not want to wind up like that. Yes, she was making big money, but she was lonely and tied to her job. I wanted freedom. The idea of going back to an office full-time made me want to throw up.

Then something interesting happened. As the weeks went by, the gushing at the office over my dessert samples transformed into disinterest, then resent. My voicemail filled up with frustrated pleas and complaints: I was not keeping up, I was never there when they really needed me, this part-time thing was a little too inconvenient for them.

And that was that. It was a mutual breakup. Yes, it was scary going back out there. But if leaving New York for London had taught me one thing, it's that I was going to be all right.

So I made a break and started pitching myself again—this time to digital agencies, which in those days were the new kids on the block. People in traditional print and broadcast advertising thought it was a risky move. But I knew better, and this was just my style.

Scouring trade journals as I did during those heady early

days, I sought out the movers and shakers—mainly the movers, because it meant they were leaving a gap at their old agency, and potentially hiring at their new one. Two for the price of one. I convinced people to try me out despite my relatively insignificant online experience, and I learned that my people skills and sheer persistence counted as much as, if not more than, my ability to craft a headline or a call to action. Soon, I was free-lancing again all over town. I was booked solid and sometimes had to take a break from one job so I could get my foot in the door somewhere else. I started expanding my portfolio beyond beauty brands. Banking, technology, charities, fashion, food, travel—I did it all—except for tobacco, which I had always found incomprehensible well before smoking was banned in public places. I just couldn't see the allure of smoke, unless it was used to preserve salmon.

Leaving the agency was the right move. And I was having so much luck online professionally that I figured I should give it another shot—in the romance department.

PIECE OF CAKE

I HAD TRIED online dating back in New York during my extensive dry spell after The Boyfriend, but it was pointless, as I was nowhere near over him. Now in London with my shiny new life, I was optimistic about the prospect. And this time, I had a specific idea of what I wanted in a mate. I understood the perils of being picky, but if the internet was swarming with thousands of new prospects, I could surely afford to be a tad selective.

I got a profile on Soulmates, the dating site from *The Guardian*. The newspaper was bound to have a good mix of candidates who were intelligent but not snooty, thoughtful but not obstinate, broad-minded but not unscrupulous. I didn't think I was asking for too much. And indeed, I met a couple of contenders. Sadly, they didn't ring my bells. Until, that is, I came across The Conquistador. Unbeknown to me, he was seemingly on a quest to explore the dating territory in more ways than one.

I liked his profile so much that I had broken "the rules" and emailed him first. When I didn't hear from him, I took it as a sign that making the first move sends you straight to the email rubbish bin.

Then two weeks later came the breezy reply. The Conquistador had been in a skiing accident and was recovering at his mother's home in Yorkshire. A perfect recipe for runaway fantasizing. I would picture him typing from his bed, his leg in a cast elevated precariously above his head. A wounded hero in my mind, we corresponded feverishly for three weeks as he told me about his physical therapy sessions, his doting mother and sister, and his favorite book: *Wuthering Heights*. He had traveled far and wide and was well-versed in food and wine. He owned his own flat in northwest London. To top it off, he spoke Spanish. This was everything I needed to know. The Conquistador was my dream *hombre*.

Every day, several times a day, we'd exchange exhilarating, poetic missives. He told me about his eventual return home and the pains he was going through to get "round" on crutches. He was hungry for tales of my Cuban upbringing and details of what I was baking in class. Our emails felt like choreography, and I found myself completely swept up in a dance that made me delightfully dizzy. Meanwhile, I started rereading Brontë—and compulsively checking The Conquistador's profile. I redirected my nervous energy to the Stairmaster at the gym, where I pounded out my increased carbohydrate intake and smiled while pondering what I'd write to him next.

We agreed to meet, and on the appointed day I was so giddy, I could barely concentrate in class while we made St. Honoré Cake, a layered, cream-filled bonanza of puff pastry. Named after the French patron saint of bakers and pastry chefs, it's sinfully elaborate and contains enough sugar to warrant a confession—presumably why it's dedicated to the heavens. The Conquistador, by now relying on a single crutch, joked that I should be able to identify him by his sword. I swooned.

As was usually the case after class, I went home with the entire cake and started plotting ways to get rid of it. I had learned my lesson to share the results of our labor right away, or I ran the risk of upgrading to a larger uniform.

A lightbulb went off.

"I think I'll give him a slice," I thought to myself.

Yes, this was perfect! It would be such a sweet culmination to our courting correspondence. How could he resist?

As any good Cuban girl would, I called my mother to make sure it was a smart idea. My mother normally doesn't tell me what to do. She is constantly encouraging me to trust myself, something at which I really should get better. But this time she thought the nutmeg had gone to my head.

"¿Estás loca?"

Was I crazy?

I told my mother that if I were meeting any one of my friends, I would obviously be sharing my cake with them. In fact, I thought it was rude not to take a slice for him to try. This was a completely friendly gesture, nothing more. In hindsight, I could see that I was guilty of that single-woman crime: trying too hard. On top of that, I wanted to show off.

"I don't think it's a good idea," she warned, "But you do whatever you want."

I hate when my mother is so level headed.

As I boarded the double-decker bus en route to the pub where The Conquistador would be waiting, I held the paper bag containing my bait. I pictured his eyes growing wide with delight when I passed it to him, and I envisioned us telling this story for years to come. Yet when the moment came, The Conquistador barely muttered "thanks" and looked like he wanted to get the hell out of there.

Immediately, I wished I'd listened to my mother. I had gone too far and assumed way too much. I looked like I had an agenda. Why, oh why, do I think of these things much too late?

The Conquistador tried to suppress his discomfort with a

bottle of Rioja when we ventured to a nearby tapas place. Nervous, I started talking and drinking too much.

But just when I thought my cake was a dreadful mistake, the Rioja started working—on him. Now he was in confession mode. He told me about the string of women he had been involved with online—or, rather, off. He boasted how he had told one woman that he wasn't looking for anything serious, yet she was so into him that she insisted she would be happy with a fling.

"She called me one night and said she really just wanted sex, but I knew she wanted more. Otherwise I would have come over."

What a gentleman.

A week later, after a few follow-up emails and texts that went nowhere, The Conquistador bowed out:

"I enjoyed meeting you, and thank you for the cake. But I get the impression you're looking for something a lot more serious than I am at the moment."

At the moment. It was so cold and clinical, as if he were diagnosing me with some kind of affliction for wanting to have a real relationship.

Pardon me, *señor*, but the site is called Soulmates, not Serial Seducers.

I can make fun of it now, but my *corazón* was successfully slain for about three months after that single encounter.

I pulled my profile from the site and focused on another pursuit: Serpentine, London's most popular running club.

FLESH, BLOOD, AND MOZZARELLA

SERPENTINE RUNNING CLUB is named after a lake that snakes through Hyde Park, right in the middle of London. Every Tuesday night we'd meet for a run, then head to the pub.

"Personally, I'd be thrilled if a woman brought me a slice of cake on a date."

The Triathlete laughed as he said it.

Was it a hint? There hadn't been any kind of romantic chemistry that I noticed, at least not on my side—which might explain why I felt I could tell him the story in the first place.

Like me, he was a vegetarian. This was my second attempt at vegetarianism since The Boyfriend when, not wanting to rock the boat with the man, I gave up the meat. Back then, I went to great lengths to conceal this inconvenient truth—namely from myself—even going so far as to write an article about vegetarian teenagers that conveniently resulted in my being so moved that I decided to join their cause.

I obviously didn't do enough research, because in the next year and a half, I put on about 10 pounds. I had merely replaced meat with cheese. Lots of it.

The episode culminated with The Boyfriend and I

devouring a disgusting bucket of fried chicken from a sad shack on a dusty road in the depressing depths of Bergenfield, New Jersey—once labeled "Teenage Wasteland" by the Village Voice newspaper. Let's just say it wasn't the brightest time in my life.

A year before I moved to London, I started experiencing pretty severe acid reflux. Heartburn—how fitting. So I decided to go vegetarian again. I became the picture of healthy eating, filling my fridge with all sorts of colorful things, keeping a tub of nuts and seeds on my desk, and discovering the joys of vegetarian cooking around the world. I was eating and exploring in such a way that made meat-based cooking seem quite limiting.

Nobody thought my "phase" would last in London, but it flourished. I'd ignore Rosie's jibes about my "green and brown food," annoying her with, among other things, a soy version of bangers (sausage) and mash. But not Spotted Dick—a pudding of dried fruit that was probably dreamed up in a pub at closing time. Sorry, can't do it. I even went vegan for a while, which really did it for Rosie. Soon, though, she became addicted to my avocado-cucumber maki and asked for a lesson. And there, in her sausage-stocked kitchen, we bonded while sealing seaweed around vegetables and rice.

As a vegetarian, I actually took pleasure in my narrowed choices. I'd look for the "V" on the menu, and that was that. Instead of feeling restricted, I felt liberated. I chose to be content with my vegetarian options, much like those in an arranged marriage choose to accept their spouses. Instead of lamenting what you're missing, you emphasize what you're getting.

Then I visited France. I tried to be veggie—I really did—and admittedly subsisted mainly on pastries and caramels when I realized the sorry state of *cuisine végétale*. But after my third consecutive dinner of cheese ravioli, I demanded the fish special. After all, *poisson* sounds very much like passion, and I simply couldn't resist.

In London, being a pescatarian seemed to suit me just fine, until I started waking up thinking about pepperoni pizza.

I shared my carnivorous cravings with The Triathlete, and we decided to go for it. This was deliberate, mutual. He was such a great guy, and heck, if he could do it, so could I. He pedaled half an hour in the rain to meet me at La Porchetta. By the time he got to the place, he was so soaked he had to borrow a T-shirt from one of the waiters.

I braced myself for the experience. I didn't recognize myself as I ordered pepperoni. Its spicy scent arrived first, and as the waiter brought the pizza—speckled with so much pepperoni it nearly obliterated everything else—I wondered how my body and palate would react to this now unfamiliar indulgence. And you know what? As with many things you build up and wait for, it was, in the end, no big deal.

Between bites, I was gauging my feelings for The Triathlete. He was cute, he was nice, he was employed, and he was making a real effort to see me. Yet, to my intense frustration, I did not feel attracted to him, and no amount of bonding over pepperoni was changing that.

Meanwhile, The Barrister had joined our running club, which meant a steady weekly slot when I could both get my hopes up and get rejected.

Crushes are like cravings. Why do we desire what isn't good for us? I don't know about you, but I don't get sudden pangs of longing for steamed broccoli.

I believe there's a fault in the wiring of the sexes. If you think about it, we should be programmed to be attracted only to those attracted to us. It makes sense for the propagation of the species. Isn't unrequited love a major drain on procreation?

Aye, there's the rub. Love. When it comes to making babies,

all you need is lust. Which is why modern romance can be so darn difficult. Today, we're after more than simply spreading the seed. I think The Conquistador wanted more, too. And eventually I had to admit that he probably wasn't a jerk. He just didn't crave me, cake or no cake.

WHO MOVED MY GRILLED CHEESE?

BOROUGH MARKET BECAME my favorite place to eat in London. Just opposite London Bridge station, it was open to the public only on Fridays and Saturdays and got very busy. Rightly so.

I would go there on my bicycle—a 90-minute return trip—to atone for the calories consumed in between. And there is one single item that made up for nearly all of them: THE grilled cheese sandwich.

Bill Oglethorpe of Neal's Yard Dairy had been toasting his signature sandwiches to wide acclaim for years. Mounds of Montgomery cheddar and onions barely contained within thick, buttered slices of Poilâne sourdough are pressed until molten, then tucked in a simple paper napkin. This is not the kind of sandwich you wander around the market with. It demands your full attention. I would claim a nearby stoop and concentrate on each bite, hoping someone wouldn't need me to move in order to get through the building door.

During a visit to London, Ruth Reichl of *Gourmet* magazine had one of these sandwiches—and then another—then proclaimed it "the Platonic ideal of grilled cheese." A stream of devotees followed soon after, with lines snaking past nearby Monmouth Coffee Company.

Imagine my utter shock the Saturday I awoke with visions of grilled cheese and made my journey to the market but was frozen in my impatient tracks when I saw that Bill's faithful presence was no longer. There was no stall, no Bill, no grilled cheese. I immediately walked over to Neal's Yard Dairy outside the market, and, as if I had lost a small child, pleaded with a cheese monger as to the whereabouts of my sandwich. Was Bill on a well-deserved break? Had he decided to take his stall on the road? Worse. He had been kicked out by the council for illegal street trading. I had been eating illicit cheese! The thought of it made me want it all the more.

The cheese monger clearly did not comprehend my panic. Instead of engaging with me in joint grilled-cheese mourning and detective work, he decided to return to his task of handing out samples of Brie de Meaux. Bah. I pushed my way past the tourists ogling oat cakes and tapped the guy with the Stinking Bishop (a pungent, yet mild-tasting soft cheese washed in pear cider).

Now I was getting somewhere. Bill would return, I was told, with a sanctioned stall inside the market! When? Sometime in the summer. That's all I got.

I called them every week to find out when THE sandwich would return, all the while avoiding the market as one would when a romance goes sour.

When the appointed day came, I made a beeline for Neal's Yard Dairy and asked where Bill's new stall was, then dodged spicy chorizos and £4 smoothies as I closed in on my target.

I finally found Bill at the back of the Green Market (near the cathedral), sweating over his bubbling Raclette with barely a bustling queue in front of him. For just a little while, I'd have him all to myself.

This I had control over. This I could understand. Plan for, work around. Here I felt no fear of rejection, no cultural barrier, and no longing that would go unanswered. My food haunts had become my antidote to dating.

ONE-AND-ONLY GRILLED CHEESE
Adapted from Bill Oglethorpe
Makes one sandwich

Bill's recipe is not a secret. The original contains not just Montgomery cheddar, but also Comté and Ogleshield (a washed-rind cheese). Nothing compares to the in-person experience. But if Bill's not a bike ride away, this will have to do.

¾ cup (75 g) of the best grated cheddar you can find
¼ cup (25 g) grated Gruyere
Small handful of chopped shallots
Clove of garlic, crushed
Two slices of good sourdough (from the middle of the loaf for a big sandwich)
½ tablespoon of butter for greasing

1. Pile the cheese, shallots, and garlic between the slices of bread, then place the sandwich on a hot, lightly greased griddle. Press it down with a cast-iron panini press, or use a heavy frying pan.
2. Cook for about 3 minutes until the crust starts to brown and the cheese melts through.
3. Flip and cook on the other side until golden. Slice in half and surrender.

TABLE FOR ONE

I'M A NATURAL LONER. I like people, I really do, but I also relish solitude. It comes in handy when you're an only child and do things like up and move to another country on your own. After all, if you can't entertain yourself, how can you expect others to want to come along for the ride?

One of my favorite things to do wherever I am—whether traveling or living there—is to find places to be alone. In New York I claimed one particular rock in Central Park as mine. Not far from Strawberry Fields, it was wide enough, smooth enough, and flat enough so I could sit down, pull out a sandwich, and eat in delicious near-silence. It took me a couple of years to find this haven, and it was worth it.

I'd found my hideaway in London, too: under the shade of a bushy tree in Hyde Park facing the Serpentine dotted with paddle boats. The London equivalent of my old rock in Central Park, it was entirely faithful to me and let me sit there for hours without demanding a thing. Week after week, I never found anyone else under it.

I'd head there on my bike at least once a week and usually

brought with me a brownie in a paper bag from Whole Foods—
if it hadn't yet disappeared into my belly.

I was perfectly happy being by myself—when it was by
choice. That's the difference between being alone and feeling
lonely.

My friend Jamie, whom I met in New York, likes to remind
me that I refused to share a dessert the first time we went for
lunch at a Cuban restaurant in the East Village. I argued that
not sharing this course is a selfless act rather than a selfish one—
ordering two meant there was more for everyone and the chance
to try someone else's. Yes, that was it.

And now there was even more reason for ordering multiple
desserts. Because without realizing it, I had thrown myself into
another distraction from dating: the London marathon. Having
only a 1:05 10K under my belt, I rearranged my weekends to do
the long runs prescribed in my training plan. I had discovered
that, while going to the pub with my fellow Serpies was fun, I
was a real solo runner at heart. No surprise there.

Running was a perfect opportunity to listen to music very
loudly. And to daydream—a time to concoct all sorts of elaborate
schemes and "what ifs." Sometimes I'd picture myself engaging
in a heated courtroom-style debate with The Barrister that
would ultimately explode in a Hollywood-style kiss neither of
us could hold ourselves back from (cue "Kiss" by Prince.) Or,
while playing Al Green's "Tired of Being Alone" during my
cooldown, I'd imagine The Conquistador giving in and calling
me, announcing that he'd relinquished his Casanova leanings,
seeing that he had failed to get me out of his head.

Neither of these came to fruition. Meanwhile, I had gone
from vegetarian to vacuum cleaner (or "Hoover" as they like to
call it in the UK), sucking up entire La Porchetta pizzas and
brick-sized Flour Power Bakery brownies from Borough Market.
Dense, chewy, deep and single-handedly capable of stopping

you in your market-strolling tracks, they were like flourless chocolate cake, but with more weight.

None of the calories seemed to stick. I had found heaven. A fitting payoff for those 2 ½ - hour runs and the ice baths that came after.

I finished the marathon in 5:05—an hour off my target. My favorite moment came at about mile 18. I was wearing my name on my shirt, and out of the sea of onlookers one guy popped out, got on his knees in front of me, put his palms together, and implored, "Come on, Jess, make me proud."

Guy, if you're reading this, thank you.

Shin splints had thrown off my training six weeks before the marathon, and I wasn't sure I'd start, let alone finish. Then, when I saw Big Ben come into view near the end of the course, a surge of newfound energy burst within me. Tears came quickly. I had made it, in more ways than one.

I was a Londoner. And now a marathoner. The only problem was that I continued to eat like I was gearing up to run 26.2 miles. But I deserved a little break from the training, right?

They say that for every week you don't exercise, you lose a month of fitness. Well, when you're still eating 3,000 calories a day, the effect is even more noticeable. Soon I had to wiggle a bit too much to zip up my Topshop jeans. A muffin top—and not the edible variety—was taking shape.

ALMOST BOROUGH MARKET BROWNIES
Makes 16 squares

After tinkering with various recipes, this is the closest I've come to the brownies from Flour Power Bakery.

1 stick (113 g) unsalted butter

1 cup (200 g) sugar

¾ cups (75 g) unsweetened cocoa powder

¼ teaspoon sea salt

½ teaspoon pure vanilla extract

2 large eggs

1 cup (120 g) all-purpose flour (plain flour in the UK)

1. Preheat the oven to 325°F (160°C). Butter and lightly flour an 8 x 8 baking pan.
2. Make a bain marie: put half an inch of water into a small saucepan and set a heat-proof bowl on top. Turn heat to high until water boils, then reduce to low so it simmers.
3. Add the butter to the bowl. When it melts, add the sugar, cocoa, and salt. Stir until combined and take off the heat.
4. Stir in the vanilla and eggs, then the flour until it disappears.
5. Spread evenly in prepared pan and bake 20 to 25 minutes, until a toothpick inserted in the center comes out clean.
6. Let cool, turn onto cutting board, and cut into squares. Absolutely incredible as a base for a scoop of good vanilla ice cream, a drizzle of chocolate sauce, and a scattering of chopped walnuts. Who's counting calories?

TEMPTATION, TREASON, AND TAPAS

For someone who would much rather nose around a farmers' market than a department store, tapas are exciting beyond belief. I get as wide-eyed over a plate of Manchego cheese varieties as some women might get at the sight of designer shoes.

Tapas are the culinary equivalent of a shopping spree: you really only grasp the damage once you've tallied up the individual prices and get home with a lot of extra weight. You never really know how much you've consumed. Sadly, you can't return anything, either.

And is there a more Bacchanalian cuisine than tapas? It all depends on the participants involved. If you do it right, the seemingly endless stream of bite-sized flavors, colors, and textures demands equal imbibing of red and white. Of course, half the allure is the communal nature of it.

Now that I had a hearty group of friends, I wanted to book a big table for dinner, just like I loved to do in New York. Choosing the cuisine was easy. But was I going to remain faithful to Navarro's, my usual tapas haunt, or stray somewhere new?

Navarro's on Charlotte Street had been a steady on the top tapas list since 1997. It was old-fashioned and festive in the kind of way you expect Spanish restaurants to be. It knew how to push all the right buttons with satisfying classics like *champiñones al ajillo* (mushrooms in garlic and rosemary) and *bacalao a la roteña* (stewed cod.)

But there was a new place just down the road I had stolen more than an occasional glance at: Fino. With its swank cocktail bar and basement restaurant, it seemed everybody wanted Fino's "modern" tapas. And now so did I.

I booked a table for 10 at Fino. Seven women, three men. Most were fellow runners. All were single. That higher men-to-women ratio I had heard about was not evident here.

We staggered the men around the table and, already slightly lightheaded from the sangria, I asked if there were any special requests. Then I ran down the menu, asking for two of this and three of that, wielding my Spanish for effect.

Glancing diagonally across the table at The Barrister sitting there in all his devastating confidence, I felt the urge to throw caution to the wind.

"I just want to kiss him," I whispered to Isla, one of my Serpentine buddies. Isla is Scottish and worked as a buyer for a fashion label. I love her style, especially paired with her down-to-earth demeanor.

"Oh Jess, I think you should find someone else to kiss," she replied in an apologetic tone.

Wait, what? The circuits in my brain fired rapidly, trying to compute this revelation. It was a revelation, right? She clearly knew something.

Had The Barrister confided in her that he thought I liked him, and—worse still—was he so annoyed by it that he had enlisted her to dissuade me?

I felt the heat of embarrassment fill my cheeks, but there was no time to think.

Queen scallops arrived on rows of seashells resting atop salt, a dish fit for Botticelli's Venus. The usual *patatas bravas* (fried potatoes) were reincarnated here as thick, garlicky sticks with a side of hot sauce. The cod showed up in the form of breaded, round croquettes and tartar dip. *Tortillas* (omelets) were stuffed with either spinach or chorizo. Hands crisscrossed as more than two dozen plates danced over the table. There is something about eating with a group that infuses the experience with a devil-may-care attitude.

Now onto dessert.

This had become a rampant affair. And if it was going to be new, hell, it was going to be different. Out went the traditional *flan* and *crema Catalana*. "A round of white and dark chocolate shots!" someone yelled. The lack of restraint was contagious as the last course appeared. Out of the corner of my eye, I could see The Barrister getting cozy with the woman next to him. Spoons floated in flights of ceremony over the plates, dipping into the warm chocolate fondant with pistachio ice cream here, and the stack of sugar-dusted doughnuts there, before the raspberry shortcake was thrust into the center of the table, punctuated by restrained sips of the layered liquid chocolate and mouthfuls of the dessert wine.

Modern love or old-fashioned romance? When it came to tapas, I didn't have to choose.

And I could forget—for a few moments or hours—what felt to me like the random luck of love. I was ordering it, but it wasn't coming. I knew what I wanted on the menu, but it seemed to be reserved for a select few. Yet surrounded by single friends, I felt safe. Normal.

I looked around the table—at all these people I never would

have known had I not taken a leap of faith and moved to London. I had created this new life out of thin air. And it was delectable. Even if, by the end of the night, The Barrister had his brawny, sculpted arm around someone else.

SECOND COURSE

THEY SAY TOM-MAH-TO, I SAY TO-MAY-TO

"It's maths, not math," said The Accountant on our second date at a little Mediterranean place in Fulham Broadway.

I had just finished telling him I was never good with numbers, but that I was very comfortable with words. And he comes out with this.

I looked at him with displeasure.

"What's the matter?" he said, taking another large sip of his third drink. "If you're here, you need to learn to speak proper English."

I had met The Accountant at a nightclub—where you have to go if you want to stay out late in London, as the pubs all close at 11 p.m. It was the first time in a long time I had been excited by someone who had asked me out.

Until now. His tone had suddenly gone from adoring to condescending, and I did not like it at all.

I pushed my reservations aside. He was a real gentleman, and Charlie approved of him. So did her now-fiancé. Yes, it turned out that a guy could spend the night with you, mutter "see you around" the next morning, then a year later ask you to marry him.

All in all, there were so many pluses to The Accountant. He appreciated my food obsession. In fact, he was kind of in awe of it. And of me.

I made a picnic for him; he cooked us a fish dinner out of a cookbook. He'd surprise me with bagels and coffee from a French press in the morning; I'd impress him with my sushi and desserts.

"Jess! You're such a gem. I should start calling you Gemma!"

He told me this was the happiest he'd been in years.

Things were going as well as I could expect with The Accountant, so I did what seemed perfectly natural to me: I asked him if he'd get a blood test. Even with a condom, I wanted to be extra cautious.

Looking back, I see that this was a total rookie move—and completely counterculture. Safe sex did not get nearly the amount of mention in the UK as it did in the US. I learned this from a British colleague when she excitedly told me that she had hooked up with an old pal she bumped into on the way home—in the park. She giggled about the fact that her knickers (panties) were still hanging from a tree.

"What, you just did it right there?"

"Yes!" she squealed.

"Without, you know, anything?"

"Well, yes. There was no time to get a condom."

My attention first fell on the way she pronounced it: "kun dum." There was a musicality to it, the way Rosie would say "Bar-bay-duhsss" instead of the American "Bar-bay-dohse" when talking about her next "holiday."

Then I took it in: the blatant nonchalance toward casual

sex. I'd only ever slept with The Boyfriend so far, and it was only after I made him get tested, and when I was certain we were a steady item. One-night stands totally blew my mind, and not in the way you'd think. I just didn't understand them. If I liked a man enough to sleep with him, I liked him enough to have him around for more than one night.

And now here was The Accountant. Things were far from perfect, but it had been over five years since I had broken off my engagement and been with anyone. With the appearance of The Accountant, I now had a live one I actually liked who liked me back, and I was going to make this happen, dammit.

So I asked for the test and, to my surprise, he happily complied. A week later he sent me a text saying his results were negative. This thing was on! The euphoria of breaking my dry streak and being in a real relationship lulled me into believing everything was finally working out. The Accountant and I went away on a romantic "mini break" outside London. Perfect. And in the "safety" of the test result, I decided not to bother with protection.

Then a seed of doubt made itself known in the pit of my stomach.

Suddenly I realized I really didn't know this guy very well at all. We'd only been together two months. Could I trust him? I was on the pill, but what if he had an STD?

I needed to see the results on paper. Yet I also knew that whether he was telling the truth or not, my launching into a dating version of the Spanish Inquisition would spell the beginning of the end.

To my horror, he couldn't produce the evidence. Clearly flustered, he told me an elaborate story about his doctor's office having lost the records and promised me he'd go for another test. I was relieved. Sort of.

I wished I could be as carefree about sex as my colleague, but I wasn't. I was a complete mess, obsessing over the potentially disastrous implications of my unprotected encounter.

One night, after finally managing to fall asleep, I woke up to the tap, tap, tap of water coming down from a leak above my bed. I put a stockpot under the crack when I first caught it, only to find out that my room was directly under the water tanks. The landlord patched it up, and things seemed fine for a few days.

Then everything came crashing down. I awoke to the sound of someone pounding at my door. It was my downstairs neighbor telling me that water was seeping into his flat. The water pipes had burst. My living room carpet was soaked.

That afternoon, The Accountant called to say he had something to tell me. Two fears ricocheted in my mind: that he had some dreadful medical information to disclose, and that I was going to be alone again—this time with a terrible disease that prevented me from being with anyone else.

I waited for him at home. When he arrived, he wouldn't even take off his coat.

Standing and barely making eye contact, he silently surveyed the water damage.

"I don't think I can be a good boyfriend to you," he said. "I just don't see a future together."

Then he asked if he could have his stuff.

I sat on the couch motionless. Inside, I was angry and afraid.

"I scheduled tests for both of us," I said flatly. "It's at the sexual-health clinic in Victoria. Next Tuesday. You'd better meet me there."

I knew it was over. Now I just needed to take care of myself.

He walked out the door and I just sat there, staring at the drenched carpet. The irony of the situation was not lost on me.

The Accountant did meet me at the clinic, and he held my hand in the waiting room before we were both called in separately.

Looking down at his fingers wrapped around mine, I felt resigned and confused. He didn't have to hold my hand. He could have been livid, making me feel like a naïve fool for creating this drama in the first place.

Instead, he was supportive and agreeable—what I wanted in a man. But I was almost certain he had lied to me, and about something important. I couldn't reconcile these opposing qualities.

On the way out, he asked if he'd ever see me again.

"I'll give you a call, and I hope we can at least be friends."

"What's the point?" I asked.

He shrugged, and I watched him disappear into the Underground.

A grueling wait of a week later, the tests all came back normal. Once the internal chaos of waiting subsided, there was a vacuum, and grief quickly filled it. I tried to make sense out of experiencing both happiness and heartbreak within the space of three months. I would recall his words. Two conflicting messages played over and over in my head: "This is the happiest I've been in years" and "I don't think we have a future together."

Had I been wrong? Had I put too much pressure on him, on myself, and on the relationship by wanting us to move into more intimacy so quickly—and especially after I'd been alone for so long? Maybe I was guilty of the same thing with The Conquistador—putting so much stock on that one date that desperation and impossible expectation poured out of my pores and turned him off.

I admonished myself for demanding and expecting too much, for getting it all wrong, for not having a clue about how any of this dating stuff worked.

The Boyfriend had been so sure about me—about us—from the beginning. Maybe he was an exception to the rule. Apparently, I was not going to have another guy declare his undying love for me within the first few weeks. Clearly, I had no idea what a normal courtship was supposed to look like or how a healthy relationship was supposed to work. It had nothing to do with a negative blood test.

Yes, I had become a Londoner, but I felt like such a foreigner to this thing called being human.

I could have sunk into despair, but I had to find a new place to live, and quickly. So I moved into a big one-bedroom flat in Kensington—with hardwood floors.

BREAKFAST AND THE BREAKUP

AFTER MY BROKEN engagement to The Boyfriend, I emerged from a sea of tissues and endless whys clutching my Mastercard on Manhattan's Fifth Avenue. I resolved that my inability to let go could only be remedied by one thing: a piece of fine jewelry I would buy for myself, to replace the diamond solitaire ring I hadn't worn in over two years.

And so through the revolving doors of Tiffany & Co. I pushed, rushing past giddy brides-to-be who were ring shopping with their doting banker boyfriends. The slim, black-strapped watch wrapped my left wrist perfectly, and I knew: it was time to move on.

My disentanglement with The Accountant was less severe and saw me descend into the basement of Selfridges for a Bodum coffee press. I'd gone from a furnished apartment to a completely empty one, going all around town picking out furniture and building my arm muscles hauling tableware to my new place. I was, in essence, buying my own bridal registry. Meanwhile, I ate grilled-cheese sandwiches and plain rice until my kitchen was fully set up. I was getting good at starting from scratch. For the first few weeks, I slept on a mattress on the floor, alone. I was good at that, too.

Which got me thinking about the lessons we learn from relationships—especially the failed ones.

I learned many of my lessons at breakfast. A handy-dandy one I picked up from The Boyfriend is how to crack an egg with one hand. It doesn't really move things along any quicker and involves an element of danger, so you do this only in front of other people to show off. I, for one, was impressed. Crack after crack, the yolks would remain intact under his hand. Tellingly, the same could not be said for the two of us.

Another revelation from The Boyfriend was that the perfect pot of coffee comes not out of a pot but a press. It looks nice at the breakfast table, too.

Breakfast is also a crucial way to gauge a date's potential, although granted that if someone is actually in the kitchen with you in the morning, then we would assume there is promise. On a more advanced note, we come to the Spanish omelet—*Tortilla Española*. If you're going through the trouble of chopping and frying to make this, only to have your companion lean over the skillet and say, "You're not really going to feed me onions this early, are you?" it's gas off, game over. I learned this one too late —it's what The Accountant said when I made it for him.

TORTILLA ESPAÑOLA FOR TWO
Adapted from my Aunt Carmela

2 medium roasting potatoes
1 tablespoon olive oil
2 tablespoons butter
1 small Spanish (yellow) onion
6 large eggs

A bunch of flat-leaf parsley, stemmed and finely
chopped (about ¼ cup)
1 ½ teaspoons sea salt
Black pepper

1. Scrub and cut the potatoes into ½-inch pieces.
   Place in a roasting tin (pan), toss with the olive oil
   and ½ teaspoon of the salt, then spread in a single
   layer.
2. Bake at 400°F (200°C) until golden (about 35
   minutes), stirring halfway through so they don't
   stick.
3. When the potatoes are almost done, put the butter
   in a heavy oven-proof 8-inch skillet and turn the
   heat to medium-low.
4. Peel, halve, and slice the onion into ¼-inch slivers,
   then add to the pan when the butter melts. Cook,
   stirring frequently, until translucent and just
   starting to color (10 minutes).
5. In a bowl, lightly scramble the eggs with the parsley,
   1 teaspoon salt, and generous grindings of black
   pepper.
6. Add the potatoes to the onions, stir, and cook for
   another minute. Pour in the egg mixture.
7. As it starts to cook, use a spatula to gently coax the
   sides of the omelet toward the center of the pan,
   allowing the uncooked egg to run down the sides
   and into the bottom. Cook until mostly set.
8. Pop the whole pan under the broiler, and grill until
   the top is nicely golden. Keep a close eye on it; if the
   edges start to puff up like a soufflé, press them down
   with a spatula.
9. Cool slightly, flip onto a plate, and cut into wedges.

SO MANY CHEFS, SO LITTLE TIME

I WAS LOOKING FORWARD to it the way some women count down the days to the Harrods annual sale. For weeks I had read teasers in the papers, building the momentum and my appetite. Taste of London.

The event happens only once a year. Like many food festivals, once inside you'll need to buy currency in the form of "crowns" for food and drink. It's somewhat like shopping in a foreign country and makes you spend just as much. Clever of the organizers, isn't it?

When you have 40 top restaurants from which to sample in a pre-appointed four-hour time slot, you need a strategy. I didn't have one. The only thing I knew was that I wanted to try whatever chef Tom Aikens was serving. His cute freckles and mop of ginger hair had made him the pretty boy du jour of the restaurant scene.

So, a stack of crowns in hand, Margaret and I decided to let the nose be our guide and were soon wooed by the intensely fragrant rice noodles with chili, prawn, and coconut sauce from Pan-Asian eatery Nahm. Garnished with a bright spray of fresh herbs, it was the kind of simple yet tantalizing thing you'd expect to get from a street vendor in Thailand, but better, and just as hot. By the time I slurped the last noodle, my lips were tingling. I needed something sweet.

And what do you know? Tom Aikens was at the next stand. His mango rice with mango parfait and mango mousse was the gustatory equivalent of pouring ice water on a burn. The triple layer of textures and flavors—cool and tropical mingling with creamy and calming—turned out to be my favorite taste of the evening.

The Cuban in me was excited to see mango popping up in various menus throughout. Mango is the only non-chocolate thing that will satisfy my sweet tooth. As I was swooning over Chef Aiken's mangoes, Margaret slyly poured me another glass of champagne and convinced me to go talk to him under the guise of getting an interview for the food blog I'd been writing. I was so nervous that I dropped my crowns and notepad before I even uttered a rushed, shaky word, but the famous chef was incredibly charming and helpful. The man earned two Michelin stars before he was 26, yet there was no attitude. He made me feel like I was the only one in the room or, in this case, Regent's Park.

Where was I? Ah, yes, the food. After I bumbled some more, Margaret and I stumbled over to the Cinnamon Club stand for Bengali-spiced crab cakes. A surprise ingredient—beet-root—bled beautifully and sweetly into the fresh, meaty shreds.

There were a few specialty vendors on hand. I'm always on the lookout for great bread, especially rye, and most definitely sourdough, so I had to pull over for the wheat-free loaves at Breads Etcetera.

I couldn't decide which I loved most. Was it the dark, dense Danish Original, the softer loaf infused with black olives and herbs de Provence, or the Nutty Original with walnuts and a touch of dark treacle? Nuts won, if only because it would make a great match for the jars of peanut butter and jam in my fridge.

They say it takes 20 minutes for your stomach to tell your brain it's full. Well, we had been sampling for three hours, and my belly still hadn't gotten the memo.

Moving on, I was briefly hypnotized by the shiny Valrhona hot chocolate fondue swirling at Boxwood Café until I saw a plate of fish and chips from Canteen floating by. I can never resist the dish and just had to find out if it was better than at my local pub. 10 crowns and two bites later, sadly it was not.

This unfortunate lapse was quickly made up for by a happy reunion with fried baby squid at Fino, salty and crisp as if you had pulled them from the sea just like that.

The glorious, still-lit British summer evening was deceiving —it was nearly 9:30 p.m. and time to go. A word of warning about those crowns: I got so carried away that even I—a petite woman with an appetite to challenge a footballer's—had a ton of them left over and ended up exchanging them for a bottle of Sauvignon Blanc.

But I wasn't complaining. And, save for a disappointing brush with fish and chips, neither was my stomach, which once again transferred a clear message to my brain, and now to you: this, my friends, was Great (Food) Britain—and I was in love with it.

MY-OH-MY MANGO MINT SALAD
Serves one

So simple yet spectacular. Make this when the mango's perfume can't be missed, and not a day sooner.

3 large lettuce leaves

1 tablespoon flax oil
1 teaspoon apple cider vinegar
Half a ripe mango, peeled, pitted, and chopped
4-inch cucumber portion, halved and thinly sliced
A handful of mixed sprouts
A handful of hazelnuts, chopped
A few sprigs fresh mint, torn

Arrange the lettuce leaves on a plate. Whisk the oil and vinegar together, then toss with remaining ingredients and arrange atop the leaves.

ON WASABI

"LET'S GET A TRAILER. You and me, like white trash. What do you say, baby?"

I was at a rodeo-themed barbecue, and a hammered Canadian came out with this. We were both wearing cowboy hats.

I had found him incredibly sexy up until this point. His comment was a total turn-off. Besides, he wasn't single, so I wasn't going to go there anyway.

"And your girlfriend too?" I lobbed back.

"Yeah baby, her too."

Girlfriend or not, I was not getting in a trailer—or anything else—with anybody.

Springtime flash floods had given way to heinous heat, which is somewhat preferable, if I could actually lie in the breeze under a shady tree. But no, I was a sniffling, snorting, sneezing mess. And I can assure you that the only white lines I do are in the form of buttercream piping. I am talking about the hideous little monster known as hay fever.

I foolishly thought that, having reached the month of June with no allergy symptoms, I was going to experience this

English summer without it. But I was wrong. So there I was, at a rodeo barbecue on a cocktail of antihistamines, Sudafed, and allergy eye drops. I was actually doing OK until it was time to go outside for the barbecue. A flurry of tissues, gradual reddening of the nose, and nasal squeak of my voice were drawing attention from the rest of the party. The unattractiveness of it was of no consequence. The real issue was that I had to keep my mouth at a constant gape in order to breathe. And with my sense of smell blocked, the daunting realization that I would be unable to fully taste my food was too much to bear. I had to leave.

Depressed and hungry, I sat dabbing at my nose on the crawling Northern Line—and reading *The Man Who Ate Everything* by Jeffrey Steingarten—when, suddenly, I remembered something at the back of my alphabetized spice drawer. Just the thought of it filled me with glee. Wasabi. Also known as Japanese horseradish, the sharp condiment was the only remedy that would do the trick. A feast of sushi rolls composed itself in my mind and, as if by magic, the familiar sensation of salivation returned as I anticipated an extra-strong dose of the green stuff.

Once home, I immediately got to work, making the sushi rice that would be seasoned with vinegar and mirin, then patted onto nori sheets and rolled around cucumber matchsticks, avocado slices, and snips from a pot of chives. I cut each roll into bite-sized pieces, set them hurriedly on a rectangular ceramic sushi dish, then sprinkled them with toasted sesame seeds of both the black and beige varieties. Yes, all this pomp and circumstance so I would have something to dunk in a (matching) little ceramic dish holding a generous amount of wasabi mixed with soy sauce (I can't stand toothpaste-style wasabi and always get mine in powdered form). The Japanese, who use wasabi quite sparingly, balk at this, calling it "wasabi soup."

With all due respect, I needed all the help I could get. Chopsticks in hand and tissue nearby, I dipped and ate. And waited. Sure enough, my tongue began to tingle and my nose took it in. Something was happening. And it was called taste. I could taste again!

To celebrate, I made a simple lassi with yogurt and frozen mango for dessert, and I could make out the dash of nutmeg I had put in it for kicks. Some may say that the change in location may have caused the spontaneous clearing of my sinuses. Or that it was simply a classic case of psychosomatics. This called for some investigating.

I Googled. It turns out that the heat in wasabi, like mustard, creates vapors in the nasal cavity, causing a sensation that can feel like a clearing effect. In other words, perception isn't always reality. What's more, researchers believe that it increases blood flow to the nose, making you more congested!

But it gets worse. As I clicked through pages of wasabi worship, I discovered that what I had been buying all this time probably wasn't wasabi at all. True wasabi root is rare and very expensive, even in Japan, which may explain its frugal use. What you get in most restaurants and shops is really a combination of horseradish, mustard, cornstarch, and green food coloring.

Had I been doped or duped?

With impending horror, I checked the label on the tin. Word for word, the ingredients confirmed my worst fears. I had been dealing with an impostor.

LAZY SUSHI
Serves one

When I'm craving nori (seaweed) rolls but not the rolling, I throw this together.

1 ripe avocado
2-inch cucumber portion
1 nori (roasted seaweed) sheet, cut into short strips
Handful of chives or green onions, sliced
Handful of mixed sprouts
¼ teaspoon wasabi (or more, depending on how hot you like it)
1 ½ tablespoons tamari
1 tablespoon sesame seeds

1. Use a sharp knife to halve and twist the avocado open, then use the tip of the knife to slice a grid through the flesh just to the skin. Spoon the pieces out into a bowl.
2. Halve the cucumber lengthwise and slice into thin half-moons.
3. Stir the wasabi into the tamari until it dissolves.
4. Toss everything together until the nori goes soft.

I must have been on some seriously strong wasabi when I accepted an assignment to cover Tiger Woods in England for *The New York Times*.

It all started with the 2006 World Cup. I had become mesmerized by the euphoria of football (aka soccer) fandom. And there was no better place to be than at a pub when England was in the quarterfinal. Soon, my own bout of football fever eclipsed that of my British friends. One day while catching the latest match report in *The Guardian*, I noticed a call for submissions: "Send us your headlines so we can rip them off in the morning."

I had been writing my food blog ever since I started at Le Cordon Bleu, but in these past few weeks I had switched from posting about food halls to football. So I sent the editor one of my posts—"Requiem For A Team"—about the penalty shootout that sealed Portugal's win against England.

"I'd say your take is worth a fair bit," came the editor's reply. "I wonder if you'd potentially be interested in coming in for a freelance shift?

The British really can be so very polite.

Was he kidding? Of course I wanted to come in! Never mind that the only experience I'd had in reporting was a three-month internship at ABC News Radio as a sidekick to the entertainment correspondent.

I locked myself in my flat for an entire weekend and pored over the sports sections of all the major dailies, consuming a whole pizza from Basilico—my favorite almost-New-York pizza place—and two boxes of chocolate-dipped flapjacks. And it had to be Fudge's brand. These were my latest addiction—a granola bar-like concoction Margaret aptly described as "a bar of butter and sugar with a couple of oats stuck on the outside." She forgot to mention the chocolate.

When the appointed day came, it seemed I had worried for nothing. The editor gave me free rein to write two pieces on whatever I wanted, as long as I did it from an American's perspective.

My idea: to interview Jay DeMerit, an American who played for Watford, the English football club. The editor asked, "Do you know how hard it is to get an interview with one of those guys?"

No, I didn't know. I broke into a mild sweat and did what had gotten me this far: I shoved my fear aside and got Jay on the phone. I'm not sure if I was more nervous because of the editor's challenge or because Jay could double as Val Kilmer. My hands were shaking when I made the call, but Jay's familiar accent put me at ease as he talked about his boyhood dreams of playing in the Premier League.

Then I did another story on golfer John Daly about how Americans love a good redemption tale. A three-time divorcee with a history of gambling, drinking, and weight problems, his willingness to spill it all in his autobiography endeared him to fans more than ever. Confession, I argued in the article, was absolution. Americans are irresistibly drawn to penance, not perfection.

I would learn that lesson myself soon enough. But first I needed to fail—big time.

After two days at *The Guardian*, I got this silly idea that I would become a sports reporter. And I had my sights set on no less than the Premier League of reporting.

I shot off a query to the sports editor at *The New York Times* asking if he needed a foreign correspondent. To my astonishment, he replied. Could I forward some samples?

Of course I could! I sent my robust portfolio—two whole articles—and waited.

Silence. Well, that figures. I wasn't cut out.

Months later, having given up on a *New York Times* byline, the sports editor's name popped into my inbox.

"Would you be interested in covering Tiger Woods in two British tournaments, and are you available?"

Was he kidding? Of course I wanted to do it! Never mind I'd never picked up a golf club, much less read an article about the sport. But you don't say no to *The New York Times*. So I said yes. Then I said to myself, "Oh, shit."

I ran to the Waterstones bookstore on Kensington High Street and bought *Bluffer's Guide to Golf* and *Learn Golf in a Weekend*. I holed up in my flat, ate Cheerios out of the box, and got so sick with panic that I jump-started my old acid reflux problem.

Golf-speak was foreign to me. Studying the sports section made me cross-eyed.

"Rounds of 5-over 77 Thursday and 9-over 81 Friday."

What kind of math(s) was this?

It seemed that every score was multiplied by two and divided by pi, then rearranged in Morse code. Sometimes I thought I was reading haiku or *Harry Potter*: "His chances of a birdie gone, he then lipped out a 3-foot putt for par" and "Casey three-putted from the front of the green for bogey."

Or how about "He birdied the first seven holes on the back."

That just sounded kinky.

Then there were the Taoist undertones—how golf is all about being in the moment. You must think only of the present shot, not what lies ahead. Aha! Maybe this was the route I should take. I could focus entirely on the philosophy of "the green" and just sort of ignore the scoring, hoping the editors wouldn't notice.

I was desperate. There were only two days to go before the tournament, and my hotel room was booked. I was to cover Woods for the whole weekend, provided he was still "in contention."

Hello! When was Tiger Woods not in contention? I monitored the score reports, though I couldn't make sense of them, hoping for a miracle.

To my utter disbelief, Woods crashed out a day before I headed for the course. Sorry, Tiger. But now I had two weeks before the next tournament to practice my bluff. Like a college student cramming for a test, I read every golf article I could find. And prayed.

When the dreaded day arrived, I dragged my suitcase up an endless hill to the media tent at the Wentworth golf course in Virginia Water, an affluent village not far from London. Once inside, there were rows upon rows of desk space with reporters hunched over their laptops. Every single one of them was male. Only two other women had been assigned to cover the tournament. There would be one bright spot in this exercise after all: no waiting for the toilets.

I surveyed the enormous, buzzing space. Paranoia began to set in. Why were the press officers ignoring me? Could they already tell I was a complete fake? Finally, one of them directed me to a section of desk bearing a plastic sign with *The New York Times* in big, bold letters. As I sat down and unpacked my laptop, I looked over my shoulder to see if anyone was calling me out. I felt like a child who had accidentally wandered into a grown-ups-only event.

There were a gazillion TV screens and scoreboards, and the Irish reporter next to me kept looking over and smiling. I was sure he could read my mind. How was I going to get the help I needed—and fast—while concealing my rookie status? The first round was starting in half an hour, and I had no clue as to the standard operating procedure.

Then, in what felt like an outward display of my frazzled internal state, rain started pounding the tent.

"Where's your rain gear?" I asked the Irishman, trying to get a gauge on when he'd be venturing outside so I could shadow him. I was trying to act casual. That's when I found out that reporters hardly ever leave the tent. My visions of strolling around the course with my all-access pass quickly evaporated. Then a cute guy wearing a badge came over to show me how to use the tournament-tracking electronic thing on my desk.

Tech Guy didn't seem to mind my silly questions, and we chatted for a bit as the Irish reporter looked on, somewhat sourly. I was positive he'd tell on me any minute. Once my lesson was finished, Tech Guy said that a group would be getting together that night for pizza. Fantastic. That was more like it.

As soon as he strode off, the Irish reporter placed his hand on my shoulder.

"Let's go, love, think I'll catch this round."

As we made our way to the course, he introduced me to a gray-haired Scottish reporter. Now we were inside the ropes, just a few feet from Woods. He was so Nike from head to toe, it looked like he had just come out of a shopping bag. The clouds started to clear as Woods took his first swing. The first glimmers of a story started to come together in my mind.

It was all chitchat with the two legit reporters as we walked along the course. They'd obviously been doing this for eons, and suddenly I was moved to confess my virgin-reporter status. They immediately warmed up to me, and the Scotsman said I was lucky, because in American pressrooms nobody talks to each other.

We made our way to the food tent, and I got so distracted by the false sense of security of the free lunch that I got seconds, only to realize I now had a mere two hours to file my story.

When I got back to the media tent, a clock was ticking loudly inside my head. The pressure was so intense, I kept thinking someone was going to get on the loudspeaker and blow my cover. "Miss Stone, will you kindly leave the Big Brother tent—now!"

BBC Radio once did a segment on "impostor syndrome"—the name for that feeling that you're going to be found out, exposed, shamed forevermore. It's usually baseless, but not in this case. My worries were completely warranted. I was truly out of my league.

I scrambled to write my story and came up with what I thought was a brilliant line:

"A birdie on the par-4 ninth—his first of three for the round —made him even with Furyk for the round at the turn. And with that the rain cleared, sending up a rainbow that stretched over the dampened course."

I managed to file my story two minutes before deadline and handed it over to the Scottish reporter to read. He gave me a hesitant smirk. Later that night at the pub, he told me that I'd written too much about the weather. Then his Silent Bob friend from a sister paper asked me how much experience I had at this thing. My time was up. I knew it.

The pressure within me mounting to "Tell-Tale Heart" proportions, I called the sports desk. Disaster. The desk editor was absolutely furious.

"I have issues with it. You talk about the weather. I feel like I don't know what happened."

Yeah, me neither!

She said she'd call back, but she never did. I got into such a panic that I gave Tech Guy and his pizza a complete miss. I went to bed wishing I'd never had that stupid sports reporting idea to begin with.

When I woke up after a fitful night's sleep, I jumped online and saw that my name was indeed on the sports page, but this looked nothing like my story. Where was my freaking rainbow?

I crawled back to the media tent, where a BBC journalist stopped by to ask me what I thought the US team needed to do to win the Ryder Cup. Err...

I walked the first nine holes with the Associated Press guy, who for sure by then knew I was a fraud. Suddenly, lightning played overhead. A sudden downpour erupted. The round was stopped. A miracle!

I ran back to the tent, walked over to Silent Bob and said, "How 'bout that weather?"

I began several hours of mad typing to compose a story about a round that wasn't even over. I filed 850 words—100 more than what they'd asked for. Heck, they could always cut, right? After all, they'd shaved 200 words off my stuff yesterday.

Just as I hit the "send" button, Woods came in to give a press conference. Dammit.

After waiting around for a call from the sports desk that never came, I packed up. Tech Guy gave me a gentlemanly ride to the hotel so I could catch a cab to the train station, where I ended up waiting for an hour, my sense of defeat as stark as a penalty shootout. On the platform, my phone rang. It was the desk editor, wanting to know if I got any more quotes.

"There's no voice from him. Didn't you get anything else?"

I humbly ventured that the conference started late and that everything sounded like a repeat from the previous one.

"Yeah," he shot back, "Welcome to sports journalism."

He was right. I'd blown it.

But it wasn't because I'd had no idea what I was doing.

Instead, I realized that I had missed a critical point: I had been attempting to model my reporting after UK sports coverage, which was completely different from the US.

I had been lost in translation—but this time in reverse.

I concluded that reporting was as exhausting and unrewarding as dating. Once again, I was much better off sticking with food.

In a much more sensible move, I shot off a query to the food editor at *The Times*, who quickly commissioned me to write a series on soup, cheese, and bread. Three of my favorite things. Now that was a score I could understand.

TO COOK, OR NOT TO COOK

SIDEWALK FLIRTING. I mean *pavement*. It happens every day in the city: eyes darting here to there, volleying quickly or lingering for a cheeky stare. And so it was in Covent Garden, the tourist destination in the West End that houses some hidden gems for the locals—if you know where to look.

The area was home to a digital agency that booked me on a regular basis. I was now the go-to girl for translating American copy so it would appeal to British and European audiences.

Lunch was, as usual, my favorite part of the day, and I always went out—alone. On this particular outing, I had just turned the corner when I felt someone's glare. I came closer, his eyes refusing to leave me. It was Rembrandt, hanging on Rose Street. Turns out this was part of The Grand Tour, an exhibition on the streets of London, consisting of 43 full-sized re-creations of National Gallery paintings.

What kind of man would paint a self-portrait, and would you want to date him? Having just finished *Harry Potter and the Deathly Hallows*, I launched into a little fantasy of what it would be like if I could reach into Rembrandt's portrait and take his hand, leading him through my Covent Garden haunts.

Would he squeal in delight when he discovered £25 massages in Neal's Yard? Surely his muscles must be quite tense from having to pose and paint at the same time.

Once my spying Dutchman emerged, lazy and limber, I'd show him World Café, where he would offer to buy me a Turkish *mezze* platter while he, after considerable hemming and hawing, decides to go all out for the Jamaican stew. We'd share a glass of fruit-topped ginger and green tea non-dairy ice cream. Taking a spoonful, he would study the subtle shades of pastel in it before scrutinizing my profile.

But I wouldn't want my new friend to start bumping into me at my usual haunts, including my preferred Food for Thought just a minute away. That's where he'd find me forking through a big slab of spinach-and-potato quiche surrounded by crunchy greens and juicy beets. A girl has to keep certain things to herself, especially from a man who spends more time in front of the mirror than she does.

To me, New York is a diner's city and London is a cook's town. With great food at all price points to be had at any hour in New York, eating out is almost too easy. You can find outstanding restaurants in London, too, but you'll have to pay much more for the privilege. And with London's sprawl, you'll take longer to get there. Cooking is often the easier choice, especially with the abundance of international ingredients to be found.

Borough Market is as good as it gets when it comes to food shopping under one non-roof. But I wouldn't call it a one-stop shop. I'm a bit of a player when it comes to stocking my kitchen. I like to buy from a bunch of different places.

One of the things I love about London is that for the price of a cab home from the West End, you can fly to a different country in a few hours. But you can also eat like you're in Italy tonight without any of the hassle.

One day, I was feeling a little nostalgic about Florence, where I'd spent those blissful weeks during graduate school becoming well-acquainted with both Renaissance art and the art of eating. I consoled myself and tried to appease my cravings by taking myself over to the West End for an Italian delicatessen jaunt.

I Camisa & Son on Compton Street in Soho was crammed with what seemed like every kind of dried pasta shape and rice variety out there, along with sweet organic cherry tomatoes, cheery pots of fresh basil, fat balls of buffalo mozzarella, handmade potato gnocchi, and fresh stuffed pasta. I'd love to have spent a few hours in there peeking into all the drawers and reading every single label, but the shop swarmed with real Italians who looked like they knew what they were doing. I grabbed a box of dried *lasagne con spinaci* that was at eye level and quickly paid up.

Zigzag down the road to Brewer Street, and you'll find Lina Stores, where browsing for semolina is slightly less stressful. I asked the pleasant girl layering ravioli if she had skinny penne—without the ridges—and she pointed to a Barilla box by the window. I brought it over to her. Against my protests, she opened it to make sure I was buying the right one. And, what do you know—Pennette Lisce No. 69 was exactly what I was looking for.

I chatted with Tony, whose wife owns the shop, and I asked him where he likes to eat Italian food in London.

"At home, my wife," he said. "I am lucky."

CURE THE CRAVING PARMIGIANA
Serves two

It's rubbish, not trash. Trolleys, not shopping carts. Bins, not baskets. My accent was still American, but if I wanted to get up to my seventh-floor flat, I'd better take the lift (elevator). Or else I'd be left standing on the pavement (that's "sidewalk" stateside).

Not long after I landed in Heathrow in that unforgiving winter of 2004, I embarked upon an intense, fruitless hunt for measuring cups. In the UK, cups are strictly used for drinking, not measuring. And so, exhausted, I settled on eyeballing quantities until later that year when I was happily reunited with the old Brooklyn kitchen stash I kept at my mother's house in Florida. In the intermittent period, I began my initiation into the nomenclature of the British food world.

Take, for example, the first time I tried to make guacamole in London. I searched high and low for cilantro before finally taking my nose to a bright green leaf labeled "coriander." Aha! It also took a while to learn that when making pie crusts, the only Grahams you'll find in Britain are blokes (guys). Use Digestives instead, as unappetizing as that might sound.

Two of my favorite vegetables are zucchini and eggplant. In the UK: courgette and aubergine, respectively. And this is a recipe where, depending on the season, the vegetables are as interchangeable as their names have now become in my mind. You don't need to measure anything, and whichever side of the Atlantic you are on, you and yours will be eating in half an hour.

For the tomato sauce:

2 garlic cloves, peeled and very thinly sliced
A glug (about a tablespoon) of olive oil
16 oz can whole Italian plum tomatoes
Sea salt
Black pepper

For the vegetables:

2 zucchinis/courgettes OR 1 eggplant/aubergine
All-purpose flour (plain flour in the UK)—about one
cup or 120 g (garbanzo flour makes an excellent gluten-
free substitute here)
1 teaspoon sea salt
Pinch cayenne pepper
Dried herbs such as oregano, tarragon, and thyme
1 egg
Olive oil (enough to cover the bottom of the pan)
Black pepper
Extra virgin olive oil for drizzling

Dried pasta such as spaghettini or linguini (enough
for two)
A handful of fresh basil leaves, chopped
Parmigiano Reggiano cheese for grating

1. Heat the garlic and olive oil in a heavy saucepan
   over low heat for about five minutes until the garlic
   just begins to color. Watch closely; garlic burns
   easily.
2. Add the tomatoes, turn down the heat, and simmer
   for 20 minutes until the tomatoes are broken up.
   Season with salt, and grind in some black pepper.
3. Meanwhile, cook the pasta in plenty of boiling
   salted water until al dente.
4. Pour enough oil to cover the bottom of a heavy sauté
   pan and turn the heat up to medium high.
5. Cut your chosen vegetable diagonally into slices no
   more than ½-inch thick.
6. Shake a handful of flour onto a large plate, then add

a good sprinkling of salt, the cayenne pepper, and enough dried herbs so you get a nicely speckled mix.

7. Lightly beat the egg in a bowl. Dip each vegetable slice into the egg and then into the flour mixture, coating both sides well.

8. When the oil is hot but not smoking, fry the vegetables in batches, turning once during cooking. When golden, transfer to a plate lined with paper towel.

9. By this time, everything will have cooked liked a perfectly conducted orchestra. Drain the pasta, toss with the sauce, and transfer to serving plates. Layer the vegetables over. Sprinkle with the basil, grated cheese, and plentiful grindings of black pepper. Drizzle with extra virgin olive oil.

ACQUIRED TASTES

I met The Music Man during a singles wine-tasting event to which he swore his friends had dragged him. He was in a band, raced BMX bikes, and was unlike anyone I'd been attracted to before. Who doesn't have a thing for men really into their music?

He met me at the Tube station for our first date wearing a huge set of headphones as if it were a tribal necklace. He was very cool in a street sort of way—too cool for me, in fact. I suddenly felt awkwardly self-conscious and overly formal in my skin. I wanted to show him that even though I looked tame and proper on the outside, there was a rebel within. A music rebel who had queued six hours for Morrissey tickets at London's Southbank Centre and had been to a metal gig at New York's CBGB. Wait, *was* I a rebel?

Over drinks on date two, we talked about the process of falling in love with certain songs. I know, it sounds very romantic, but stay with me.

I admitted to musical infatuations during which I could easily listen to the same song over and over until, one day, I wondered what I ever saw in it in the first place. One of the earliest I can remember involved C+C Music Factory, when I subjected my poor mother to "Gonna Make You Sweat (Everybody Dance Now)" on a perpetual loop, broken up only by the screech of the tape ribbon as I rewound the song to its studio-manufactured start—again and again. There wasn't much to do in my teenage years. Then, during university ("uni" in the UK), I got my first CD player with what turned out to be a life-changing feature—the repeat-track button. For the next several months, I had Depeche Mode's *Violator* on constant loop until I could no longer look at the thorny rose on the CD cover without wanting to pluck out the last petal.

Then in college I fell in love with classical music. Hard. It was during a musicology class. The instructor played Bach's "Air on the G String," and suddenly everything changed for me. I looked around the room; was anybody else feeling this the way I was? Classical music gave voice to my emotions, and the romance has never died. I dove into it, studying music history for a year before working at South Florida's classical radio station and attending every concert I could.

But The Music Man—who deemed "God Only Knows" by The Beach Boys a "perfect song"—talked about another form of music appreciation. With his ear cocked on an open palm and his head bobbing to an internal beat (perhaps a permanent tic from his days as a DJ), he told me that many of the songs he adores actually grew on him. Imagine that. He'd buy an album, and even if it didn't grab him at first, he'd give it a chance and a few more plays. Every now and then—and here's when he removed the invisible headphone from his ear—he'd realize, "I fucking love this song!"

I was moved. Then I realized I could relate to The Music Man after all. His story paralleled how I had come to love Green & Black's Butterscotch. Green & Black's had become my favorite chocolate in the UK, but I hadn't tried this particular version, mostly because I've never really been a butterscotch fan, but also because I tend to like my chocolate dark, sharp, and unadulterated. So it came as a surprise when this milky, candy-studded bar became more and more intoxicating as I worked my way through each ribbed square.

I started to really like The Music Man, and I even burned a CD for him. Yes, I burned him a CD! He had bought me dinner twice, and I wanted to do something in return. Perhaps, I was also trying to show him that my music collection—ranging from Jack Johnson and Franz Ferdinand to The Chemical Brothers and Scissor Sisters—was well rounded, even unexpected. And that, by default, I was ... cool. He seemed pleased with the CD when I brought it along to our third date at an Italian restaurant in Soho. Or maybe—unlike a slice of cake—it didn't matter what I brought this time. Apparently, there was an unspoken rule on date three, because he then surprised me with a trick question:

"What if I asked if I could go home with you?"

I fought my inner "no" and told myself I really needed to stop being so uptight. We took a cab to my place, and I knew right away it was a mistake.

Suddenly, he seemed incredibly uncomfortable.

"How does someone afford to live here, alone?" he asked as he looked, shell shocked, around my living room. The Music Man shared a place with three other guys on the other side of town, and the disparity in our living situations hit him. He picked up an ocean-blue glass bowl—my only piece of art so far —and asked me how much it cost.

The mood had completely shifted. We may have been in the same room, but it felt like there was a vast distance between us. Still, he stayed, and hugged me all night long as we slept; that's all we did. I made him breakfast the next morning, which he graciously ate. Predictably, I never saw him again. I knew I'd freaked him out with my "posh" flat, and now I couldn't believe that everything I'd worked so hard for was pushing away the thing I wanted most.

MUSIC TO MY TONGUE
CHOCOLATE-CHUNK COOKIES
Makes two dozen

I didn't think I'd be cheating on my New York cookie if I gave it a new twist. Here, I used Green & Black's original Maya Gold (dark chocolate laced with notes of orange and spice). It's love at first bite.

4 cups (480 g) all-purpose flour (plain flour in the UK)
1 ½ teaspoons baking soda
1/2 teaspoon sea salt
3 sticks (339 g) unsalted butter, at room temperature
1/2 cup (100 g) granulated sugar
1 ½ cups (300 g) packed dark brown sugar
2 large eggs
2 teaspoons pure vanilla extract
4 bars (100 g each) Green & Black's Chocolate (Maya Gold or whatever tickles your fancy), chopped

1. Sift flour, baking soda, and salt into a bowl. Mix in chocolate pieces and set aside.
2. Using a mixer, cream butter and sugars together at medium speed until very light, about 4-5 minutes.
3. Add eggs and the vanilla, and beat for another minute until combined.
4. Turn the speed down to low and gradually add the dry ingredients, about another minute.
5. You can now bake the cookies or chill and save for

later—just roll up the dough in plastic wrap and refrigerate.

6. When ready to bake, preheat oven to 350°F (180°C). Line a baking sheet with parchment paper, or use a nonstick baking mat.

7. Scoop two heaping tablespoons of dough for each cookie onto the baking sheet, spacing the mounds apart to allow for spreading.

8. Bake until golden brown but still soft, about 18 minutes.

9. Cool on a wire rack for 30 minutes and eat to the tune of yum, yum, yum.

HARD TO GET

IT HAD BEEN a long day working on a new campaign for De Beers Diamonds, writing a guide for guys buying engagement rings. I was tired, in more ways than one.

I was walking down the high street past Waitrose, the posh supermarket I had graduated to since my frozen tortellini days. Perfect, I thought, a much-needed dose of Fudge's chocolate-dipped flapjacks.

I marched in and, after stuffing some bok choy and chives into my wire basket so I wouldn't look like a complete junkie, I headed to the biscuit aisle, otherwise known to me as cookie nirvana.

Except my flapjacks weren't there—no blue-and-white box nestled like a book in a cookie library. I pushed the others around. Perhaps my flapjacks were behind? Maybe another flapjack addict had hidden a stash in the back. Panic ensued. State of alert. There were no flapjacks, friends. No flapjacks!

"I hate this country," I thought. Yeah, the country that let me in, gave me shelter, taught me pleasures I never knew. The country that had the balls to introduce me to chocolate-dipped flapjacks and then rip them away, just like that.

I went to the clerk, trying to compose myself. He looked puzzled.

"Chocolate-dipped fudge?"

No! I explained slowly, with a twinge of mania. He tried to take me to the other end of the store. No! My flapjacks, I told him, are over there, always over *there*. Every week. Week after *bloody* week! He went to find the manager. This didn't look good. A big guy in a forest-green blazer brandishing a gadget came over. He punched some keys.

"We've just taken stock of inventory, and they may have been shifted out."

Excuse me? It was as if he were talking about Post-It Notes. Clearly, he did not understand the gravity of the situation. He didn't see that I don't ask for much, that I am a woman with needs. And that sending me home alone is just cruel.

"Sorry, I have no control over these things," he shrugged.

Sure. That's what they all say.

Earlier that week, Margaret had lent me a copy of *Superflirt* by Tracey Cox (that has to be a made-up name). The part that really got me was her advice that, instead of the old game of acting elusive, one should be very available at the beginning of a relationship. Then once you know you have your victim right where you want them, you step back. Stop taking every single call. Plead busy when invitations are issued. Be a mystery.

Think about it in reverse. Suddenly, that thing you thought was kind of cool is now the thing you must have. Let's put it into familiar terms. Say they market a new kind of chocolate—Maybe Chocolate. They send you bars and bars of the stuff. You like. So you start buying a few here and there; you don't want to go overboard. Sometimes, you even go stretches at a time without Maybe Chocolate and think you could do without it. You even check out other chocolate. Then, one day, Maybe Chocolate is gone. Poof! Just like that. You start searching all over town. You begin to see all the amazing things you never appreciated in Maybe Chocolate. Sometimes you even forget there was a funny aftertaste. And that the packaging wasn't right. No other chocolate will do. Suddenly, Maybe Chocolate has morphed into Super Chocolate.

Ms. Cox has a point.

SCENT AND SENSIBILITY

I HAD BEEN TRADING sporadic yet suggestive glances with a certain stranger in my building. Then, one morning, we spoke.

I was walking toward my bicycle, he was pumping up the tires in his—quite feverishly, I might add. There were enthusiastic hellos; I walked on and then proceeded to unbolt my bike in unusually slow motion. About five minutes later, he pushed his bike past mine; and I seized the moment, boldly asking something bicycle-related.

The conversation did not stray from this topic, and, later at the gym, I pondered the entire exchange for over an hour. I decided that he must be single, because on a Sunday morning everybody else is either still under the covers or changing nappies (diapers). Then I looked around and amused myself with the thought that everyone in the room was releasing pent-up frustration in the name of exercise.

During an exceptionally long break on the chest press, I remembered that the English poet Ted Hughes had once sent a provocative note to a love interest (not his wife) that was duly returned with a single blade of freshly-cut grass dipped in Dior perfume. Hughes sent the note back, this time with another blade of grass beside hers. Can you just die?

I started to plot. I would tie a sprig of something to said stranger's handlebars, and if he were keen, perhaps I would find it reciprocated on mine the next day. The upshot of this was that if he wasn't interested, a) there would be no way for him to know for sure that it was me, and b) I'd conclude he must be quite dull and unromantic anyway.

Now, what to use? A rose would be too obvious, overrated. And besides, it shouldn't be bought. Some weeds from Hyde Park, perhaps? Hmm, this was proving more difficult than I thought.

Once home and in the kitchen, the answer came. Cilantro was too polarizing, and it would wilt into a mushy mess within hours. Ditto dill. Rosemary, on the other hand, could withstand hurricane-force winds but wasn't very pretty. Chives—a viable contender, but there was the connection with onions.

Now basil, oh sweet basil! So bright and cheery. It gets along with everything from San Marzano tomatoes to Berkshire strawberries. What's more, he'd have to bury his nose in it, deeply.

Then I thought about the negative domestic ramifications this little flight of fancy might have if our ensuing acquaintance lasted no longer than a pile of herbs forgotten at the bottom of the fridge drawer. And that Hughes' mistress, not to mention Sylvia Plath, committed suicide. One must think long and hard before messing around under one's own roof.

I placed the pot of basil back on the windowsill, quietly.

———

It's worth remembering that even in a city as big as this, someone you know is likely right around the corner.

So it was with The Banker, a fellow expat. We first met only a few months after I moved to London. He was very eager to see me again, but I was just getting my feet wet and certainly didn't think I had come all this way to wind up with a Yank. Then we kept running into each other. To my surprise, I began to warm up to him. That's when I started to hear from him less and less. Maybe Chocolate, anyone?

I had forgotten about The Banker until I passed him on Kensington High Street near my flat. Turns out he lived just a few streets down from me. We agreed to meet at The Abingdon, where he proceeded to tell me at length about the woman who had just broken up with him.

My gut was quick to discern that all this opening up was more platonic than romantic. But when he suggested we ride our bikes to Borough Market, I let myself surrender to hope. I pictured giving him a tour of all my preferred spots, including eagerly delving into grilled-cheese sandwiches as we sat side by side on a stoop.

We did do all that, except that The Banker kept calling me "dude" and told me he'd already picked out the place he wanted to get engaged.

He had clearly lost interest, and I couldn't use the cultural excuse here. We supposedly spoke the same language. I was the common denominator in all my romantic failings. It was easy to get down on myself.

But if I flipped it around, I could see that probably none of us single people knew what the heck we were doing. I might have dismissed certain candidates right off the bat, but I had been the target of the same treatment. The closest I had gotten to a kiss from The Barrister was a drinking game at one of his parties, where we passed a single ice cube around the room from one mouth to another.

THE PROBLEM WITH PARIS

FOR YEARS I thought I'd wind up in Paris. Jackie Kennedy had been my idol in my late teens, and I wanted to speak French as breathlessly as she did. I still liked the idea, so I enrolled in classes at the Institut Français in London. Within four months, I had become more acquainted with the fillings at The Kensington Crêperie than with the verbs that filled my workbook.

Nestled in the Francophile hub that is South Kensington, the crêperie's menu is simple, and here's all you need to know: savory crepes on the left and sugary ones on the right, all served in a most charming setting reminiscent of the cafes in the Left Bank.

When a recruiter asked if I wanted to spend a week at a Parisian agency writing copy for a bilingual beauty campaign, I couldn't resist. Excited, I studied my pocket English-French dictionary on the Eurostar train and daydreamed of the bona fide croissants in my immediate future.

Yet I would quickly realize that the pleasures of Paris make Paris without romance a travesty.

It was my third time there. Yes, it was beautiful. Yes, it was delicious. But Paris has rendezvous written on every lantern-lit corner and tête à tête etched into the busiest brasserie. You must have that café crème while your legs are tangled with those of another. A playful brush of the shoe is not enough. French people don't need to play footsie. You are supposed to cross the Seine in a desperate embrace; even the dead at Père Lachaise cemetery demand a hand-held stroll.

It appeared to me that if you are lucky enough to be madly in love in Paris, restaurants and sightseeing matter little. Stumbling around together in a state of abandoned bliss seems enough from over here. I had to console myself with another kind of hot pursuit: that of *chocolat chaud*.

First stop: Ladurée. The luxury bakery is best known for its macarons. As pretty as macarons are, I've never been swept off my feet by these little merengue sandwiches. Instead, I eagerly awaited the hot chocolate, which came in a little pot and pours out silky and smooth.

Then there's Angelina, a tea room with Belle Époque decor. *Mais mon Dieu*! Creamy and thick and with hints of cayenne and cinnamon, this hot chocolate was also reminiscent of the kind my grandmother (*Abuelita*) made.

Abuelita was a charming señorita from Buenos Aires: petite and coquettish. A Scorpio in the truest sense, she wore nothing on her face apart from red lipstick, a faint sweep of powder, and the cheekiest grin. She never counted calories and made her *chocolate caliente* with butter and three kinds of milk: whole, evaporated, and condensed. My mother says I am a lot like her. That's not entirely true. I like to add a shot of Kahlua.

My grandmother would have loved Paris, and I sat at Angelina thinking about this while I tried to drink the last bit of chocolate clinging to my cup. I gave up, my gaze now locking on a pair of surprisingly familiar eyes—heavy lidded and unflinching, cutting deep and purposefully across the crowded room.

They looked like the eyes of The Music Man. Heat burst in my cheeks. Could it be?

Then I noticed the black vest over the crisp white shirt. It wasn't The Music Man. It was one of the waiters, carrying a serving of hot chocolate to perhaps another lovelorn patron.

In the same pulsating vein, attempting Paris *sans amour* succeeds in raising buried memories and the ghosts of lovers past. On my way back to London, I vowed never to return to the City of Light unless I was going with someone I was absolutely crazy about.

FLIPPING GOOD NO-FLIP GALETTES
Enough batter for four servings

When the French make crêpes with buckwheat flour, they call them *galettes*. And they usually contain savory fillings, like ham, cheese, and eggs. You can fill these with whatever you like, of course, but I happen to have a thing for bananas, chocolate, and nuts. Hold the jokes, *s'il vous plaît*.

For the galettes:

½ cup (43 g) buckwheat flour
Dash sea salt
¾ cup (177 ml) whole milk or almond milk
½ tablespoon vanilla extract
1 tablespoon maple syrup
2 tablespoons unsalted butter

For the chocolate sauce:

½ cup (118 ml) whole milk or almond milk

2 tablespoons cocoa powder
2 tablespoons maple syrup
1 teaspoon cornstarch (corn flour in the UK)
Dash sea salt

For the filling:

1 small, ripe banana, sliced on the diagonal
1 tablespoon cashews, chopped

1. Whisk together the galette ingredients (except the butter) until smooth. If necessary, add water in small increments until the batter is thin enough to pour—it should be much thinner than American-style pancake batter. Cover and refrigerate for at least two hours.
2. When you're ready to cook the galettes, make the chocolate sauce: heat the ¼ cup milk in a small saucepan. Meanwhile, combine the cocoa powder, maple syrup, cornstarch, and sea salt in a cup or small bowl.
3. When the milk starts to bubble, add a little of it into the cup and stir vigorously until smooth.
4. Add the remaining milk to the cup and stir until well-combined. Now add the sauce back into the saucepan and stir over high heat until the sauce boils and thickens. Set aside.
5. Take the batter out of the fridge and whisk it, as some of the flour may have settled on the bottom.
6. Set a large, non-stick frying pan over low-medium heat. Melt ½ tablespoon of the butter in the pan.
7. Now be quick: pour about ¼ cup batter into the

center of the pan, then swiftly lift and tilt the pan to coat the bottom.

8. Now be patient. The lower heat means the batter won't cook as quickly, but it also means you won't have to do any flipping. As the edges start to brown, use a spatula to "peel" it gently away from the pan. It's better to err on the side of crispy galettes than soggy ones!

9. Once bubbles cover most of the top, mound the banana slices onto the middle, spoon over some of the sauce, and sprinkle with the cashews.

10. Use the spatula to fold three sides in to form a triangle, or you could fold in four sides and form a square.

BAGELS AND BIG BOYS

"THE IRONY OF THE SITUATION," said Jeff, a fellow American expat, "is that you can get excellent smoked salmon here but not a decent bagel to put it on."

It was after 1 a.m. and I was at a party for Americans abroad. The festivities were coming to an end, but when a former New Yorker meets another, there are always two ways the conversation eventually goes—dating or bagels.

So far, I hadn't found a bagel in London that would match the likes of those in New York. In particular, I missed the everything bagel, sliced and sandwiched around scrambled egg and cheese.

A field trip was needed. I called Joanna, another American —we had quickly bonded over the inability to find proper Ziploc bags in the UK. The following week, Joanna and I settled in for the long ride on the top deck of the 328 bus up to Golders Green, the area in north London noted for its Jewish population.

I had heard so much about Carmelli Bagel Bakery—the most talked-about shop in the small London bagel scene—that we carried on right past the unassuming Roni's Bagel Bakery in Hampstead. About 10 northern-bound minutes later, we jumped off and made our excited trek past the Polish shops and, hold on, was that a Baskin-Robbins?

We couldn't wait to get our paws on Carmelli's bagels. Finally, it came into view, with its blue awning and big white letters. We were about to try the hottest bagel in town!

These bakeries are the fast-moving, grab-and-go kind of places. You get your bagels and you get out. Knowing we would give underdog Roni a sympathy taste test later, we ordered a single sesame bagel with cream cheese, then hurried to Caffè Nero to unwrap this baby.

Imagine our surprise when Carmelli's bagel turned out to be too tough for its own good. The bagel was dry and hardly filling; even the cream cheese was a bland disappointment. "Hot stuff" Carmelli left us cold. All talk and no show! We'd been taken for such a ride. Could we ever trust a rave review again?

We got back on the 328. After all, a girl has to eat, and we still had an appetite, Carmelli or not. We were doubtful, though. How exciting could Roni's bagels really be?

Once inside the cozy shop, we immediately felt at ease. It was welcoming and warm; and within two minutes they brought out a tray of fresh, hot bagels. We bought a half dozen and ran to Costa Coffee. Despite the arctic winds on the way, our bagels managed to stay steamy. The delicate balance of density and sweetness was ever present in this bagel—the closest I'd come since those New York days. Roni's Bakery had won us over, and completely unexpectedly.

It was comforting to know that a fine specimen of a bagel—poppy, sesame, onion, or plain—was only a bus ride away. Yet the everything bagel evaded me still. Did that elusive pearl of style and substance—bagel and beyond—exist in this town?

The case continued.

There was another reason I was carb loading: I was yearning to be near the water and decided to join a rowing club on the Thames in Hammersmith. Our clubhouse was used as Gwyneth Paltrow's office in the movie *Sliding Doors*. The movie is a close approximation of my brain, which is always wondering how life would have turned out if I had made a different decision.

When it came to rowing, I was a little apprehensive about my choice. I'm 5'1. People like me don't usually row; they cox. I was lucky that the president of the club was on the short side, so he humored me.

I quickly fell for the sport. The meditative, metronome rhythm of rowing. The sunrises on the water. The camaraderie of the crew. The concentration of testosterone. It was also grueling work. The fittest I've ever been. And the most frustrated. How come I could run a marathon, but my erg tests (those torturous sprints on an indoor rower) were still so much worse than everybody else's—even when the coach cranked up Kanye West's "Gold Digger" while getting in my face pushing me to give it my all?

Simple: sometimes size does matter.

With so many men around, you might think finding love at the boat house would be a piece of cake. Instead, I got an education in attachment—or lack thereof. It seemed to me that men are born with another, not so obvious, apparatus. I'm talking about the switch. You know, the emotional one they can turn on and off—quickly. I was going over this with my friend Dennis, the only other Cuban American I've ever known in London. We met at the beginner's rowing class, and he alone understood how bizarre it is for a girl from Miami to find herself floating on the Thames.

Dennis had moved to England years ago after running away from home to be with a man. He told me the story as we were having lunch at Whole Foods in Kensington—he, a burrito; me: brown-rice sushi. Dennis was very excited about his latest love interest, a Scottish guy, even though he had gone through an ugly breakup just a few weeks ago. I wished I could get over things like that.

"You girls analyze far too much. We find it easier to move on."

I'm about to walk over to the gelato counter. I ask Dennis what flavor he wants, and he tells me to surprise him. Astonishing. I could never leave such a thing up to someone else. Holiday destinations, pieces of jewelry, burial plots maybe, but my ice cream flavor? Never.

You see, Dennis has the switch—the attachment switch. He doesn't get as attached as we do, because it's biologically built into him not to. Survival of man depended on non-attachment. No point standing around waiting to see what the big bear was going to do or why he did it. This also explains their single-minded focus. We women, however, were back at the hearth, mashing the maize, suckling the babies, and concocting whatever hijinks must have been needed to keep the hunter bringing back his kill and our feed.

I'm standing at the gelato counter. I've looked at the creamy clouds of color many more times than I'd like to admit, and Dennis' scoop comes easily: passion fruit. It makes me think I should try something new. Come on, Jess, you can do it. Just this once. You can have the usual next time. Nope, it's my standard —one scoop chocolate, one scoop coconut.

Having left New York for London, I was clearly open to

trying new experiences. But when it came to my romantic relationships—and my ice cream—I had trouble letting go.

Turns out I wasn't the only one, and attachment wasn't black and white. Because months later, Dennis was so broken up when his boyfriend left, that he could barely eat.

LUCY, I'M NOT HOME

It happened every morning during elementary school, just after 6 a.m. I would sit at the dining table, my back to the kitchen light so as to temper the shock of premature awakening, with a big mug of *café con leche*. Eyelids at half-mast, I'd stare blankly into the thick, camel-colored infusion of full-fat milk and strong coffee. As I tipped the mug toward my mouth, the movement of the drink reminded me of the tide and the warm beaches nearby. Eventually, it coated the inside of the mug with a foamy veneer. Then I'd lick as much of its sweetness as I could before my mother—whose name really is Lucy—would remind me, for at least the third time, that the school bus would be along at any moment.

Coffee is a big deal for Cubans, and we start young. It's not exactly an ideal breakfast even for adults, but my mother was just doing what her mother did, and what her grandmother did before that. And well, I'm still here, so it couldn't have been all that bad.

Besides the daily wake-up call, there was coffee after every meal: *"un café"* or a *"cortadito"* (literally: "cut" with a splash of milk.) We make it in an espresso maker (*cafetera*) on the stove. And we add sugar. Lots of it. But not just dumped in, and definitely not in cubes. We have a ritual: you put several spoonfuls of the white stuff into a big cup; then you prepare the *cafetera*, turn up the heat under it, and watch.

As soon as the coffee begins to flow out of the top, you quickly pour a bit of it into the cup. Then you stir it vigorously with the sugar until it forms a creamy paste that goes paler the more you beat. It's like creaming butter. Once all the coffee has brewed, you mix it into the sugar paste. What you get is a heavenly head of *espumita* (foam). When you divide the coffee into the requisite shot glasses, the result resembles mini pints of Guinness.

In London, I always got my java from Monmouth Coffee, where the knowledgeable staff will grind up samples for you to try on the spot. I was particularly fond of the Guatemalan beans, especially the ones from Finca Culpan with their aura of darkest chocolate. In a completely unintentional yet blatant violation of my Cuban heritage, I'd skip the *espumita* in favor of a scant teaspoon of sugar. Sometimes I'd even have mine with soy milk. Outright *sacrilegio*.

Cubans—especially our elders—are passionate people. Anything that goes against the grain elicits shock and is on par with an act against God. Like a hurricane alert cutting into your *telenovela*. Or leaving out the *espumita* in a *café*. The same goes for the food that was trying to pass as Cuban at La Bodeguita del Medio in Kensington.

When I told my mother I was going to the restaurant, she responded with a flurry of stories about the original La Bodeguita del Medio in her native Havana. "Let me know how the *platanitos* are," she told me.

Platanitos? What *platanitos*? No *platanitos* at La Bodeguita del Medio. No *arroz con frijoles*, either. Or *palomilla*. Or *tostones*. Or *media noche*. Or anything remotely resembling that which I happily grew up on in Miami, really the only place for Cuban food outside Cuba, although New Jersey might try to argue.

Studying the menu, I grew from perplexed to downright annoyed. Quesadillas? Did they think we're Mexican? Nothing against Mexicans—their cuisine is one of the most vibrant and satisfying around. But Cuban it's not. And tapas? Wrong again, amigo. No problem with tapas, either, not at all! Just not when I want a big plate like my grandmother made. And what's this here? Poached pears? You must be joking. Where's my *flan*? The *pudín de pan*? My *natilla*!

There were four of us at the table, and we decided to share a few dishes. After about an hour, enormous plates with tiny food on them came out. Popcorn strewn on ceviche. Popcorn on fish? I'm not quite sure how this classifies as Cuban, or anything else for that matter. Then there were empanadas with a surprising side of guacamole (I see we're back in Mexico now), and mini omelets arranged like Stonehenge. I don't mind fusion, but if you're going to call it Cuban, then keep it Cuban. And keep popcorn off it either way.

OK, let me tell you how it is. Cubans love food and cooking, but the art in Cuban cuisine is in the taste, not the plating. We want masses of rice and beans. We want fried plantains heaped in a mound and placed in the center of the table for everyone to share. We want a basket of *pan Cubano*, toasted in a press until little bubbles form on top. A simple salad of avocado with onion slivers, olive oil and, vinegar. That's it.

The right Cuban restaurant would be a comfy diner with generous portions and a respect for simplicity. Stop it with the gourmet! Enough of the fusion! Cubans reserve pomp and circumstance for weddings and funerals, and a *joie de vivre* to make the French jealous. The best Cuban joint is unfussy in a *mi casa, su casa* sort of way. The original La Bodeguita del Medio was just that—a corner store in the middle of the road where you'd stock up on staples like rice, beans, plantains, and *cascos de guayaba* (guava in sugary syrup), along with mango and mamey, another tropical fruit often used in thick milkshakes. It later became the home away from home for dishes like *puerco asado, ropa vieja*, and plenty of freshly caught *mariscos. Nada más y nada menos*—nothing more and nothing less. La Bodeguita del Medio is sacred. If you're going to take the name, you had better revere it.

(La Bodeguita del Medio in Kensington didn't last very long and was replaced by a French bistro, which was actually quite good.)

CUBAN 101

Platanitos (plah-tah-nee-toes): very ripe plantains cut on the diagonal and fried until caramel in color.

Arroz con frijoles: (ah-ros kohn free-hole-less): white rice with black beans spooned on top.

Moros y Cristianos (more-ohs ee krees-tee-ah-nos): meaning Moors and Christians, or beans and rice cooked together.

Palomilla (pahl-oh-mee-yah): a very thin steak large enough to blanket your plate.

Tostones (toes-ton-ehs): green plantains, squashed with a *tostonera*, twice fried, and seasoned with salt. Often drizzled with mojo (moe-hoe), a garlicky sour-orange seasoning.

Media noche (meh-dee-ah noe-chay): meaning "midnight"—a traditional sandwich of pork, ham, cheese, pickles, and mustard on sweet toasted bread eaten at any time of the day.

Flan (flahn): milk-and-egg dessert made in a caramelized mold. My aunt Carmela always has one of these waiting for me when I visit Miami.

Pudín de pan (poo-deen deh pan): the Cuban version of bread-and-butter pudding.

Natilla (nah-tee-yah): vanilla pudding, but creamier and dusted with cinnamon. Sometimes presented in a bowl lined with ladyfingers.

Pan Cubano (pan coo-ban-oh): a very long white loaf with no nutritional value whatsoever. Often found sandwiched around *palomilla* (see above), tomato slices, onions, and shoestring potatoes.

Puerco asado (poo-er-co ah-sad-oh): pork, often roasted whole. With more garlic mojo.

Ropa vieja (rope-ah vee-ay-ha): literally "old clothes." Shredded beef stew served on white rice.

Mariscos (mah-rees-cohs): seafood, whether grilled, stewed, breaded, or fried.

BRING-ME-BACK BLACK BEANS
Serves eight as a side dish
or four (generous) portions as a main course

These are the real deal: the *frijoles negros* I grew up on in Miami, the kind my family always has bubbling away on the stove in preparation for any feast, even Thanksgiving. This recipe has all kinds of quirks and special touches passed down from my grandmother and vetted by both my mother and aunt, so try it first as it is and then adapt as you will.

1 pound (454 g) dried black beans
1 large Spanish onion, quartered
1 large bell pepper (my mother uses green, my aunt likes red), seeded and quartered
5 garlic cloves, peeled
1 bay leaf
4 tablespoons olive oil
1 teaspoon dried oregano
2 teaspoons sea salt
3 ¾ oz (106 g) jar Spanish olives stuffed with pimientos
4 oz (113 g) jar sliced pimientos

1. Rinse the beans and cover them with water in a lidded pot (the beans will swell).
2. Add a quarter of the onion, a quarter of the bell pepper, two of the garlic cloves, and the bay leaf. (My family doesn't bother cutting up the onion, bell pepper, and garlic pieces.) Soak for at least seven hours or overnight.

3. Leave the beans in the soaking water (add more water if needed so that there is an inch of water above the beans) and put the pot over high heat. The lid of the pot should be slightly askew to let out steam. When the water boils, reduce heat to keep the beans at a simmer for an hour and a half, or until the beans are soft. Stir every 20 minutes so that the beans don't stick to the bottom of the pot. You may need to keep adding water so that the beans are covered.

4. Meanwhile, make the *sofrito*: finely chop the rest of the onion, bell pepper, and garlic cloves (you can use a food processor).

5. Put the olive oil in the skillet and turn the heat to medium. Once hot, add the *sofrito* along with the oregano and cook until onions are soft but not brown—about ten minutes.

6. When the beans are soft, add the *sofrito* along with the salt. Simmer—uncovered—for another 10-15 minutes, stirring frequently until the beans are very soft and the "soup" has thickened. Use the back of a wooden spoon to smash some of the beans against the side of the pot to thicken the mixture even more.

7. When the beans are done and your house smells like Havana, take the frijoles off the heat and stir in the olives (including the liquid) along with the jarred pimientos (yes, you want olives with pimientos and then more pimientos). Taste and add more salt if desired.

8. Serve alongside white rice and fried plantains.

The following week, I take a train up to Scotland and meet Isla, the fashion buyer and running-club friend. She has invited me to spend Christmas with her family.

It has been nearly a year since The Accountant and I had our dramatic blood-test breakup. That's when the text messages started—first quite casually ("Happy Christmas, Jess!"), then outright nostalgically ("You are a very special person, and I'll never forget the time I spent with you"), and finally, an invitation for coffee.

When the texts first came in, I didn't know who it was; I had deleted his number from my phone. But he had obviously kept mine.

The Accountant's return caught me by surprise, but my reaction was even more surprising to me. I declined to meet him. It was flattering that The Accountant held no hard feelings—and perhaps even wanted to try again—despite everything that had happened. I had spent months lambasting myself for having created the whole situation to begin with. But I was now in a much better place—literally and emotionally—and didn't feel the need to re-engage.

Meanwhile, Isla couldn't take her mind off this one guy who seemed absolutely perfect for her.

"He was listing all the qualities he likes in a woman, and I realized he was describing me!"

But there was an issue: the perfect guy had a longtime girlfriend. Still, Isla was convinced this was *the* guy for her. She knew it in her bones.

I suggested, "What if you could put him out of your mind for now, because you knew he would be ready for you by this time next year?"

Seeing how The Accountant had come back after I stopped thinking about him, Isla decided to try. It was better than pining for him anyway.

And if it turned out that he wasn't the right guy for her, she wouldn't be wasting her energy on him.

Seemed so simple. If only I knew how to keep taking my own medicine.

MORE THAN A MOUTHFUL

WHAT'S the price of not listening to your gut?

During the winter of 2007, it cost me exactly 250 British pounds. That's when I experienced my intoxicating infatuation with The Secret Agent.

He earned his nickname because of the clandestine, enigmatic way he conducted his interactions with me. I met him at a bar where Margaret had organized one of her gatherings, and I was in an especially good mood. An article I wrote about aphrodisiac foods had just been published in a London daily newspaper. I showed up at the bar with the paper rolled up under my arm and a big grin on my face.

This newfound confidence must have been attractive, because almost as soon as I arrived, two very nice guys approached me. We started chatting. Then I happened to notice a third had entered the conversation and was just, well, staring at me without saying a word.

Being the American that I am, I stuck out my hand, readjusting my claim to fame under my arm, and said, "Hi, I'm Jessica."

"I know," he said flatly, the side of his mouth lengthening into a smirk.

I cocked my head at him. "How?"

"We met at Margaret's birthday drinks."

Oh. That was a few months ago. I honestly had no recollection, which seemed to entice him all the more. Before I knew it, the two other guys ducked out of the conversation, leaving me alone with The Secret Agent.

He asked me what dating was like in America and told me he hadn't been on a date in over 10 years.

"How do you get together with women then?" I asked.

He smiled and raised an eyebrow.

"I just snog them."

The Secret Agent somehow managed to corral me from everybody else at the bar that night, ensnaring me in a private chat full of suggestion and intrigue.

I would normally join my friends on the dance floor, but it was as if my feet had been glued to the floor in front of this man. Raising our voices over the music, we talked about body language, and the secret signals we send when we're interested in someone. Here's a useful insight I had recently learned and just had to share with him:

If you want to know if someone likes you, casually glance at their feet. If they're pointing toward you, even from across the room, it's a good sign. When someone isn't into you, they'll actually turn one foot away from you, creating an exit point. The body reveals intention, even when we think we're smart enough to hide it.

No doubt about it, The Secret Agent and I were completely

square with each other, the tips of my black boots aligned toe to toe with his. There was no misunderstanding this body language; the energy between us was so magnetic and intense, I felt us pulling toward each other.

He talked to me about his plans to travel later that year; I told him I wanted to write a book called *The Jump Factor*.

The Jump Factor, I explained, would be inspired by Malcolm Gladwell's *The Tipping Point*. While that book examined how certain ideas spread like wildfire and many more fizzle, *The Jump Factor* would redefine chemistry, uncovering why only some people make us sizzle while the rest fail to turn us on.

I've always been intensely intrigued by that elusive and intangible phenomenon called chemistry. How someone can spark outrageous flames in your heart while another won't cause so much as a flicker is fascinating to me. And the fact that the person who ignites such passions in you often turns out to be far from one's idea of perfect fills me with awe for the mysterious workings of human nature.

"I think it should be called '*The Lunge Factor*'," he said, cutting me off.

That's when I first sensed a slight tightening between my chest and my stomach. I knew this was going to be trouble. But I was too far gone.

It couldn't have been his looks. They hadn't made much of an impression on me before, even though he was clearly very handsome. It was more about this captivating confidence he had, but not like The Barrister. This was a bravado that shook me to the core, a sort of ... danger. And outright cockiness.

The Secret Agent let drop a couple of unflattering remarks about what he called "alpha males." I ignored yet another twinge of discomfort in my gut, mesmerized instead by his smirking, sexy mouth. I didn't know then that one of the quickest ways to learn everything you need to know about someone is to pay attention to the words they use when describing other people. *He* was the alpha male.

The Secret Agent excused himself to get another drink at the bar but didn't offer me one.

Margaret came over to check on me.

I chatted with her and let myself sway to the music, well aware that he was watching me.

———

Hours later, still at the bar, we discovered we were born only a few days apart.

"You know what they say about two Scorpios," I told him. I could feel the flirt in me rising up again, and I inwardly cringed as I watched myself resort to astrology.

"What's that?" he asked, taking a long sip of his beer and biting his lower lip.

"It could be either really good ... or really bad."

Now I was really going for it. Suddenly, he went quiet and stared at me again.

"I quite like you. I really want to snog your face off." He lowered his voice as he said it, but it was still forceful.

This is not exactly how I pictured things. Snogging my face off did not sound romantic, but I was trying to let go of preconceptions.

"Say that again," I quivered, knowing full well what he'd admitted.

He leaned in and repeated it in my ear. Slowly. The warmth of his breath shot throughout my body.

"Where?" I blurted.

Looking around the crowded room, I didn't want a kiss to happen there, in front of our friends. Maybe we could sneak outside to some quiet corner.

"Well, you said you live in Kensington, right?"

I was shocked. He thought he could just go home with me.

"I meant nearby—*in the vicinity*," I said, exasperated by the mechanics of this and annoyed by his defiance.

"Grab your coat," he ordered.

No man had ever talked this way to me before. He was really talking AT me. Part of me was aghast and enraged by it, but still I found myself unable to pull away.

As if under a spell, I distractedly said goodbye to my friends and fished for my jacket. I pushed through the crowd and into the bathroom to do a quick check in the mirror, then I rushed back out and down the stairs. There was no sign of him. I felt a chill down my spine. I can't believe it, I thought. He's gone. Another one—gone.

I went outside and spotted a few more people from our group, but not him. Then something made me whip around. And there he was: leaning against a signpost with his arms crossed and a very composed look on his face. So confident, so sexy.

"Didn't you say you were going to kiss me?" I managed to ask.

I hadn't planned the words. There was no planning here. I was operating on pure animal instinct.

And then he leaned in, right there in front of everyone.

"That was nice," I said, catching my breath.

He stared. And smirked some more. Saying nothing.

"Jess!" I was jolted out of my trance. Friends were waiting for me with a mini-cab. It was my only ride home. The Tube had long stopped running for the night, and a bus would have taken ages.

I jumped in the car, my mind whirling. One of the nice guys I'd been chatting with at the beginning of the night was already inside the cab, being the perfect gentleman, trying to make small talk, doing everything I wanted a man to do to make me feel safe. He was the opposite of dangerous. But I had checked out, feeling the buzz charging through my body more and more with each London roundabout.

The next morning, my excitement and anticipation were intense. To work off the energy, I put on my running shoes and headed toward Kensington Gardens. "Would he track me down? I didn't even give him my number! Would he have the foresight to look for my article, find my blog, and email me? What if he thinks I'm not interested because I ran off?"

What if, what if, *what if*.

These maddening questions bounced around my brain like ping-pong balls while I ran faster than ever to the dance beats in my earbuds. And when I got home, there it was. It popped out at me as if in blazing neon lights: an email with the subject "Lunge Factor." I held my breath and clicked on it.

"So when can I see you again?"

That's it.

No "Hey, Jess, nice meeting you last night."

No greeting, no closing, no XXX, no nothing. Just straight to the chase.

A few days a later, I was standing in the Asian-foods aisle at Tesco when my phone buzzed. It was a text from *him*. The packets of rice noodles I was carefully comparing seconds before were instantly relegated to background noise.

He wasted no time with his message:

"I want to buy some prints at The Tate for my new flat on Saturday. Want to help me?"

I immediately called Joanna, my American friend.

"Oh my God!" she yelled.

Jo was so excited I had to pull the phone away from my ear. They probably heard her all the way over in the mile-long crisps (potato chips) section, where they sell hundreds of perplexing flavors, such as "prawn cocktail."

Like me, Jo was also under the delusion that if a man invites you on a home-decorating date—and at an art museum—the next logical step is a bridal registry.

"I know, I think I've finally met SOMEONE!" I gushed.

"Ohhh, when is it going to be my turn?" she whimpered.

If it can happen to me, I told her, it can happen to anyone.

While I counted down the days to our first date, I was caged adrenaline.

The euphoria in my body was both exhilarating and frightening. I organized the entire contents of my flat. Cleaned the few pieces of silver I owned. Washed my hairbrushes. And makeup brushes. Emptied the fridge. Vacuumed inside the closets. Bought a new outfit. Did sprints in the park despite the winter chill.

This Scorpio was ready for her Scorpio. Tick tock, tick tock.

In what felt like months later (although it was only three days), I boarded the Tube wearing skinny jeans, a wraparound sweater, knee-high boots, my mother's camel-colored coat from the '60s, and a matching beret from a New York street vendor.

I had checked with The Secret Agent to find out whether he wanted to meet at The Tate Modern or The Tate Britain. It was Tate Britain, which I had not yet been to, although I knew that I would not be focusing too much on the large collection of Tudor paintings housed there. Sitting on the train, I was too antsy to even pull out the book in my purse, as I normally do. Instead, I wanted to make sure I didn't miss Victoria station where I needed to change to another train headed to Pimlico station, which was still a 7-minute walk to the museum.

It was a cold afternoon, but I could feel myself on the verge of sweat. I went up the stone steps and looked around. I was early. I sat on a bench, trying to act normally. I wondered what he'd do when we saw each other again.

Then he emerged. That's what he did—he *emerged*.

I had built him up so much and given him the starring role in my life that there could have been a red carpet at his feet. Had I passed him on the street, I may not have given him a second look. In fact, that's exactly what happened when we'd met the first time and I had forgotten him. This time, my mind had set the stage, and he was playing his part exactly as cast.

He walked right up to me, grabbed me, and kissed me.

Despite the automatic familiarity, there was a palpable awkwardness. We wandered through the exhibits absentmind-edly, making small talk. Then he casually reminded me that in the autumn he was planning to take a sabbatical and travel for a few months—alone.

Right. I had sort of forgotten about that—ignored it, the way I ignored my misgivings at the bar. Somewhere at the back of my mind I thought this meeting would change everything. That it was the happy ending I was looking for—a love story that started with me writing about aphrodisiacs and ended with him realizing I was the only thing he craved. I had begun packing my bags in my mind, imagining us traveling together. After all, I was a writer and could take my show on the road.

Was he reminding me about his trip so I wouldn't get any ideas? As I started to ponder this, he told me he'd made reservations at Hush, a swanky central London lounge/restaurant. He'd planned the whole evening, which further fueled my fantasy that this was going to be special—that *I* was special.

"For someone who hasn't been on a date in a decade, you sure know what to do," I said.

"I know, I'm starting to impress myself," he replied.

I can't remember what we had for dinner.

We moved into the lounge and sat side by side.

"Your eyes," he said, "I could just keep staring into them."

"Then don't stop," I murmured.

I was in such an altered state that I could see only his face while everything else blurred into a watercolor, like the Turner paintings we had given a passing glance in the museum. I couldn't believe that someone so alluring was interested in *me*. In his gaze, time and space disappeared. I'd never tried drugs—not even a joint—but I just *knew* this was what it felt like to be high. This had to be real, right?

He invited me back to his place and I declined, saying maybe next time. As much as I wanted him, I also wanted to figure out what his intentions were. I needed to know how much he wanted me. I wanted to believe that I had sparked something new in him, that I wasn't just one of the many girls he had snogged.

As we stood waiting for my bus, he hugged me the entire time. I breathed a momentary sigh of relief.

After another kiss, he pulled me closer and said, "You're just my size."

FEED ME LOVE

"Meet me at the Zetter on Friday at 8 p.m." flashed on my phone.

Dating The Secret Agent was like being on a scavenger hunt. I was on edge, always waiting for some kind of clue. There were no phone calls, no email volleys during the week. Only sporadic texts—brief ones.

When another text came through—if I was lucky—I could do nothing else other than go out and run three miles to release the anxiety.

He seemed to be conducting a sort of Pavlovian experiment on me, giving me just enough intermittent attention while keeping me at a distance. And I was letting him.

I told myself that his cryptic communication style was a sign of confidence. Everything about him was cloaked in mystery. I felt like I was dating James Bond. It was as if we were conducting an affair—so secretive and inscrutable, not even I knew what was going on.

This only added fuel to the fire. The attraction I felt was so powerful that my appetite disappeared. I'd make banana pancakes, have a couple of bites, and be done, a sign that something was seriously wrong. Typically, I'd polish off a stack. Normally a very sound sleeper, I would spontaneously wake in the middle of the night, eyes wide and with astonishing amounts of energy even though I was turning into a waif. Meanwhile, I was losing myself, arranging everything in my life around The Secret Agent.

While we were bowling one night, I asked Margaret what she thought was going on with me. She watched me pick up the heavy ball as if it were a feather and answered, "Dopamine." This crush had set off the feel-good chemicals in my brain, causing me to experience a natural high.

That episode taught me something I'd always sensed. For me, food—and especially sugar—is my stand-in for love or the promise of it and all the good feelings I associate with it. When I was looking forward to a date with The Secret Agent, it fed that particular hunger at the bottom of the addiction, the kind of insatiable appetite that no amount of food will satisfy.

Our dates were a week apart, with hardly any communication in between. That seemed odd given the intensity of our connection, but again I brushed it off. I wondered why he'd ask me to the Zetter, a restaurant on the other side of town, yet I went anyway.

This was our second date. He held my hand over dinner, but the mood was stilted, and I got that awful feeling that something had shifted—you know, when someone just stops feeling it for you and everything seems like it's slipping through your fingers. And the most painful thing you can do is hold on.

Then he said something completely unexpected.

"I bought some eggs and bacon for the morning."

He dropped it into the conversation, just like that.

I was taken aback, on various levels. First of all, we had only kissed, and now he was insinuating that we were spending the night together.

Second, I thought that over dinner I'd sensed him pulling away.

Had I imagined a diminishing interest? This didn't make sense.

"I'm sure your flatmate will appreciate them." The words came out before I could stop them, and I laughed nervously.

I wasn't sure if I was more disgusted by his arrogance or dismayed that he didn't seem to really like me all that much anymore, despite wanting to go to bed with me.

The bill came. Last time, he snapped it up. Tonight, he let it linger.

I dreaded this part of dating. Whenever the bill was brought to the table, it was as if a stadium-sized spotlight was suddenly focused on that piece of paper. I never knew what to do.

My unsettled energy spilled out in the form of distraction. I suddenly became aware of a familiar song—"Last Night a DJ Saved My Life" by Indeep—playing in the background. The Secret Agent recognized it too and started mumbling the words.

Unable to stand the tension between us, I offered to split the bill.

"Are you sure about that?" he asked wryly.

I wasn't sure about anything.

He didn't mention breakfast again and walked me to the Tube station, where he told me I should plan the next date. Next date? After the confusion of this one? Was he really a jerk just trying to get me in bed? Or was I blowing things out of proportion again? Was this a total cultural misunderstanding?

If perception is reality, I wondered how another woman would experience this exact moment. Margaret, I thought to myself, might not have been attracted to The Secret Agent in the first place. Isla, I was certain, wouldn't have taken any of this so seriously or put this guy on a pedestal. And I was willing to bet The Secret Agent would be more respectful of them instead of playing them like an old song.

I was stuck in my head, with painful, twisting thoughts that kept me from enjoying anything. In this moment, I wanted to be any woman but me.

I got on the train, completely dejected.

Back on Kensington High Street half an hour later, it was a little before 11 p.m.

I began the eight-minute walk back to my apartment building with my head held low and my music for company. "Tempted" by Squeeze played loudly into my earbuds. My small black purse dangled from my arm and swayed rhythmically with each step. The bag was vintage Gucci—a birthday present from Daisy, a journalist who had mentored me in Miami. I never would have bought it for myself, and I had kept it all these years. Feeling the cold air, I zipped up the top of my Agnès B. black-and-white houndstooth coat.

Still stunned by how the date had unfolded, I was barely aware of anything or anyone else. I was such an easy target. Because then a hooded thief came out of nowhere, snatched my bag, and kept running. By instinct, I shot after the man, yelling loudly and following him before he disappeared into an alley. That recurring dream I always had about not being able to scream was a lie. I could scream.

Then it hit me. I couldn't keep going after him. This wasn't safe. Realizing that I was a block from home with no way to get in or call for help, I started to cry.

A black cab pulled up and gave me a free ride to the police station, where I dutifully cancelled my credit cards and took care of business. I did it all so calmly that suddenly I had this thought: "I'd make a good mom." In that moment, I equated getting stuff done in the middle of a shit storm as being a good mom. It's not far from the truth.

I called a locksmith, who finally unbolted my door at 2:30 in the morning. As he worked on the bolt, I told him about my date. He shook his head, saying that a good guy wouldn't let me walk home alone, that he'd never have done that with his wife. Then he handed me a bill for £175. Add the price of dinner and the amount I spent on a bikini wax (just in case), and you can see what I mean about how expensive not listening to your gut can be.

The worst part is that all I could think about was that my phone was gone, and that meant The Secret Agent couldn't get a hold of me.

I started doubting myself again. Was I making too much of this? Were my expectations unreasonable? Maybe I messed things up by splitting the bill. Margaret said I was sabotaging. That I was sending mixed signals, and he could not win.

The truth is that I was sending mixed signals to myself. Why was I still interested in a man who kept me at arm's length? Why was I so intent on doing all "the right things" when he wasn't perfect, either?

Not wanting to appear dramatic, I sent him a short email downplaying the mugging.

"Thanks for a nice night. Just wanted to let you know my purse was stolen on the way home, so my phone's out of commission."

His reply barely expressed concern. Instead, he seemed annoyed. "Shame to hear it. Well, like I said, you go ahead and plan the next date."

However halfheartedly, he wanted to keep going; and, despite the awful feeling in the pit of my stomach, I wasn't able to stop myself.

He suggested Feb. 15, completely bypassing Valentine's Day. Margaret warned me that if I called him out on it, The Secret Agent would be gone for good. I tried to pretend I didn't care, but when he came over to pick me up, I couldn't mask my growing disappointment. I had to mention it.

"I don't believe in Valentine's Day," he said.

I felt my senses shift into an even higher state of alert, but I was not prepared for what came next. He announced he was going on a business trip the following week and planned to stay with an old flame who was now "just a friend." My heart dropped deeper into the recesses of my being. When we had met at the bar a few weeks earlier, he had mentioned this woman. She was one of the people he had become romantically involved with—without actually "dating" them.

It was obvious to me now that he wanted to send a clear message that I was not the only one. But did he have to be so cruel? Yet I persisted, like a dizzy moth to a flame, being even more cruel to myself.

"I don't want to get hurt," I said as we walked from my place to The Abingdon, painfully aware that I was creeping into needy mode.

"It's your choice," he said dryly.

As we sat down to dinner, he looked amused by my dismay.

"Should I take the knives away from you?" he joked.

I began downing the red wine, trying to numb the surge of emotions welling up in my body.

"Look," he said, "You're really hot. And you're nice. But I've only known you for three weeks."

He took a generous, knowing bite of the roasted Cornish hen. I poked around at my grilled salmon. His compliment wrapped in rejection obliterated my taste buds.

Somewhere in the middle of dinner, and seizing an opportunity in my wistful eyes, he changed his tune.

"Do you want to get married?"

"Someday," I said, trying to play it cool.

"Do you want to have kids?"

"Yes."

"Do you want to move back to America?"

"I don't know."

Thinking he was now getting closer to me and that he was coming around to the idea of a relationship, I asked him the same questions. His answers came in rapid fire.

"Definitely want kids. Not fussed about marriage. Don't want to move to the States."

What game was he playing? And, more importantly, why was I still there? These were the important questions, yet I was powerless to ask or answer them at the time.

I declined dessert and, against my better judgment (again), I let him stay over.

———

The next morning, feeling a false sense of intimacy, I blurted it out:

"You really never want to get married?"

That was the nail in the coffin, even though the rotten stink of this non-relationship had been around well past its expiration date.

He reminded me about his sabbatical and said that he promised himself he "wouldn't let anything" hold him back.

"But what if you really like someone?" I asked, tears gushing down my face as he got ready for work.

"That's not in the plan," he said coldly.

He gathered his things, kissed me on the forehead (the kiss of death), and walked out. No breakfast.

I went back to my room and collapsed on the bed, the beginning of a depression that lasted a good month. The pain would come in waves. How could I trust myself again? How could the chemistry I thought we had simply ... vanish? How could he just walk away after he said he hadn't felt like this in years? Does this kind of thing happen to him all the time?

I had moments of clarity, but just moments. When I separated attraction from actions, everything became clear. Except when it wasn't.

Of course, I had done it all to myself. In my head I knew my grief over this man was senseless; this was just a blip in time. But my heart ached. Sara, a senior art director I'd worked with, had once said it best: when you feel so much pain over a short time with someone, you're not mourning their loss but rather the death of a dream and all that could have been.

A few days after The Secret Agent left my flat, he sent me an email, where he briefly explained that since he would be travelling soon, it was best that we didn't see each other anymore.

The clocks sprang forward for daylight savings time, but there was no spring in my step. I'd go out to places swarming with men, but all I could see was his face. I went over and over every single word that came out of my mouth on our last night together. I thought of what I said that I shouldn't have, and what I could have said that would have changed everything. I was certain I was at fault and had come across as too needy, forcing him to walk away.

No amount of convincing otherwise from my friends helped. I had screwed things up; I knew it. I was engulfed in a trance of self-loathing, and my self-flagellation knew no bounds.

To numb the pain, I once again started bingeing on Cheerios and my chocolate-dipped flapjacks.

Not one to lock myself away, but rather living my solitude out in the world, I went to see the film *Infamous*. Daniel Craig's character said punishment was believing there was someone out there for you, then all the years go by and there's no one, and then finally you meet them but you can't have them. I made a note of that.

One day, I found The Secret Agent's cufflink beneath the sofa cushion we had sat on the last night I saw him. I couldn't bear to get rid of it. I hid it behind a framed photo of a friend's happy wedding day—out of sight but not buried, and somewhat hoping that the good vibes from that photo would finally bring me what I really needed.

I hit my preferred choice of therapy: the self-help section at the bookstore.

They say that when the student is ready, the teacher will appear.

Louise Hay's *You Can Heal Your Life* was mine. Some people discover Hay because of a medical condition. My "dis-ease" took the form of heartbreak—the kind that comes from seemingly being able to make anything happen for myself except the one thing I wanted most: love.

It wasn't until I read Hay's book that I understood exactly what was driving my move to London and even my finishing the marathon—a creative power exceeding what was in my portfolio, and one that I could call upon whenever I wanted. This inner force was always there, like the sun behind the clouds—even when I felt utterly powerless.

By sheer determination, I'd been able to create an entirely

new life from scratch in a foreign country, yet my fruitless pursuit of a lasting relationship left my heart homeless.

I tried so hard to get love that when I thought I was close, I'd be on top of the world. And then I'd hold on so tight that I'd choke the life out of any possibility, only to crash miserably on the way down. Inevitably, this approach would prevent me from acknowledging the red flags waving brightly in my face.

As I sat on the floor at Waterstones on Kensington High Street, page after page confirmed what my heart had known all along. The tugging was present from the very beginning: this guy wasn't right for me. I knew it; I just hadn't listened.

I knew that I had ignored my gut and that this was my pattern in relationships. When things didn't feel good, I pretended I didn't feel it. It was no wonder I chose men who ultimately dismissed what I wanted. They were merely reflecting that I was shortchanging myself.

I had done enough self-inquiry to know that this was rooted in my childhood—in my father's fractured presence while I was growing up. I knew that "emotionally unavailable" was as attractive to my heart as dark chocolate was to my tongue.

I was the classic case of fearing abandonment while continuously abandoning myself. I worked hard—really hard—to win a man's love, while my inner child kept crying, "Hey, what about me?"

I knew all this, but I couldn't seem to stop it. And this just made me feel worse. My heart felt like a marionette, being pulled at by whatever was going on—or not going on—in my love life.

Hay's book made me feel good. There was something so comforting in her words, so reassuring, so validating—what I had always wanted from a man but never received. Those chapters were like warm, all-accepting hugs. I would go to sleep with her words every night, often in tears.

I started to see that I was so much bigger than this one disappointment and even this one aspect of my life I couldn't get right. I saw that I was stuck in a very small, contracted space when I was focusing on this one problem.

From working on television commercials, I knew the terminology for a tight shot was "extreme close-up." That's exactly what I was doing when I let The Secret Agent's rejection define me and determine my happiness—I was giving precious, total attention to one detail at the risk of everything else. As long as I was stuck on this one detail, it's as if nothing else existed; and this is what was causing me pain. My extreme close-up on the rejection was the true cause of my distress. What's more, the thoughts I believed about this one detail could either lift me up or bring me crashing down.

Gradually, I started seeing life beyond my perceived problem. Like a camera zooming out, I opened my eyes and looked around the room—at the beautiful flat I had secured for myself, and the wondrous city outside its walls, and the friends I had made, and this dream I had created out of thin air. Look what I had done! It was no accident.

I started to feel excitement again. Everything I needed was already within me.

I had another revelation:

All through my childhood I thought I should love my father, even though he wasn't around much. Because I could have only one father, I drove myself mad trying to love him and feeling shame when I didn't. But I had a choice now. I could choose whom to love, depending on the love they showed me.

I kept reading the self-help books. There was one particular paragraph from Barbara De Angelis that somersaulted off the page at me. She wrote about how people can't give you an "injection of love," even though it may seem as if what you're feeling is coming from the outside. The other person is merely a spark or trigger for what's already inside you.

I envisioned The Secret Agent carrying a big syringe filled with love. I laughed, realizing how preposterous this was.

Then I thought of one powerful question that would completely change the way I looked at love—a question that would allow me to experience the feeling of being in love and at peace, whenever I wanted.

I asked myself: how could I experience that euphoria I felt with this guy ... without him? After all, he hadn't even been around most of the time. Our dates were a week apart. He barely even called! I had generated all those feelings of excitement and anticipation myself—he hadn't given me anything except a few crumbs. The story and emotion that sprang from it were all mine.

In a way, The Secret Agent was my savior—my encounter with him set me on my spiritual path. In trying to re-create the feelings I had "with" him, I started looking for ways to draw excitement out of everyday life. I wanted to see things differently—to truly see.

I believe it was this willingness that made everything possible. I started really paying attention to the world around me. It was much more than mindfulness. Aside from just *noticing* what was in my experience, I was intentionally drawing joy from everything I encountered.

To my astonishment, it worked. I developed an acute awareness, a sense of connectedness to everything. Things appeared hyper-saturated in color. I marveled at how much is unknown—the magic and mystery of the universe and everything in it—and it thrilled me.

Seemingly inconsequential events jumped out at me, becoming a source of delight and amazement—as if I were a child (or an alien) discovering it all for the first time.

I'd look at a dog on the street—even though I'd seen them hundreds of times before—but now I stopped to take it in. I was in awe of what made its tail wag, the sheer life force of it. When I'd go out dancing, I had to take a moment and hold myself back —I'd stand watching, transfixed by the energy in the room and the wonder of it all. The movement of the bodies, all the different faces, the music—I was blown away.

I was alive. And that was enough.

Before, I'd be scanning the room to see if an interesting stranger caught my eye. Now, everything captured my attention, but not because I wanted anything out of it. It was all for the sheer experience of being alive.

Whatever I felt during my non-relationship with The Secret Agent paled in comparison to this. This was not tinged with fear or uncertainty. This did not want anything in return. This just was. There was nothing lacking in it, because it was everything.

That experience of oneness and contentedness lasted about a week for me. But the contrast compared to what I had been feeling before was so dramatic, I'd never forget it. I had been able to alter my mood on command, without drugs, and without anything else from the outside making it happen. To be witness to this, in my own experience, was to know with utter certainty that life can change incredibly quickly—and that I can make it so. I had seen this firsthand with my move to London, but I never knew that the same could be said about my heart.

It had only been a month since I had last seen The Secret Agent, but I felt like a new person. One Saturday, I joined a few running friends at Mahiki, a tiki-themed nightclub in Mayfair.

Taking a break from the dance floor, I found myself standing next to The Barrister.

"Do you ever wonder about the universe—how it all came to be?" I asked him.

"Yes," he answered, staring into the barely lit room crowded with revelers. "But I think the real question is *where* is the universe."

I tried to wrap my mind around his answer-question and realized that, even though I could appreciate how handsome he was, I was talking to him without craving anything other than meaningful conversation.

"It's all amazing," I said to him, "Isn't it?"

THIRD COURSE

GUILTY AS CHARGED

St. Etheldreda is the oldest Catholic church in England. And there was a restaurant right on the grounds. I was sold, even though it was in Farringdon—the place where The Secret Agent and I had our second puzzling date.

The church and restaurant are nestled at the end of a cul-de-sac in Ely Place, and I'll bet many give up trying to find it. I almost did, and I was on my lunch break. There is no grand entrance. Instead, I wandered into the crypt, which, I then learned, was where Henry VIII dined at sumptuous feasts lasting several days.

The church itself is small and yet as magnificent as a cathedral, with a stunning display of stained glass that gives the place the illusion of greater depth. I noticed a rack holding books for sale in the hallway. One of them was *The Thorn Birds* by Colleen McCullough, and I chuckled at the cheekiness of whoever put it there.

After a short midday Mass, it was finally time to eat. The restaurant was tiny; it's more like a kitchen with a few tables (eight, to be exact). I was seated next to the dishwashing machine and so, by default, was almost everyone else. As I pondered the menu, I had a faint recollection from my Catholic-school days that you aren't supposed to eat anything within an hour of Holy Communion. At that moment, the priest who led the Mass walked in—robes discarded—to take his seat. Phew. If it was OK for him to eat, I was fine.

They were already out of their *plat du jour*: cod with mushrooms and spinach. I asked for the fish cake and couldn't help the offer of white wine at £2.50. I was feeling sneaky, until I caught sight of another priest raising a glass himself.

As I was waiting for my order to arrive, I inspected the surroundings from my seat. St. Etheldreda appears in Shakespeare's *Richard III*, and a quote from the play is etched on a wall in the restaurant. When I spent a semester in England during college, I had become very curious about the six wives of Henry VIII and wrote a thesis on his daughter, Elizabeth I, debating whether or not she really was a virgin. This was the summer before I met The Boyfriend, and sex—or lack thereof—was clearly on my mind.

Despite my passionate nature, my "number" has always remained low. Friends kept telling me I should just have had "fun" with The Secret Agent, but that kind of fun was just not something I was easily capable of having. It's not that I was trying to be holier-than-thou; it's that to me, sex is so great it's sacred.

As I thought of this, I peeked out the window into the cloister gardens full of bright holly leaves. I saw a giant spider web, then a second, and finally a third, each a perfect masterpiece. I wondered if the spiders nestled within noticed the others, or if each thought the spun magic was all her own. I thought of Henry's wives and how each had woven her tale.

I looked around. Every table was taken, and only a few callers were turned away at the door. How did this place not produce a queue of people?

A chat with the waitress revealed that the restaurant was part of the Bleeding Heart Restaurants for its location in nearby Bleeding Heart Yard. Legend has it that the square gets its name from the murder of Lady Elizabeth Hatton, who died following a ball at Hatton House. The guilty party? A disgruntled lover. At dawn, her body was found in the courtyard, her heart still pumping blood into the cobblestones. So they say.

My fish cake was generous and meaty, and the spinach alongside it was the leafy green color it should be. A slight pool of Hollandaise sauce let them both shine in all their glory. Finally, there was a *tarte tatin*—the French version of apple pie —very close to if not better than the one I was blessed to taste as a student at Le Cordon Bleu. I was enraptured, my pace slowing to savor every bite. I caught the waitress looking at me, and when our eyes met, we both let out a little laugh. My appetite was back.

COMING CLEAN

I'VE JUST HAD my third ice cream of the day, and I'm not in Italy. This was Bangkok, and it was oppressively hot.

It seemed that everyone in Britain had been on "hols" (holiday) to Thailand, and now it was my turn. Since moving to London four years before, I had been to New Zealand, Croatia, Greece, Sweden, and France. I had been toying with the idea of either Thailand or India when a well-traveled friend told me that if I was after relaxation, the choice was clear: Thailand.

I was apprehensive about traveling to this part of the world alone, so I booked myself on a two-week group tour and planned to have the third week all to myself. I thought that by then I'd feel more confident venturing solo.

But I didn't need the buffer after all.

I arrived a day early, and by the time the group got there, I already knew my way around, had made a few friends, enjoyed the first of many massages, and found the best place for ice cream. I don't remember the name, but it was owned by a guy named Jerk. For real.

Then there was the street food, which I had been warned to stay away from if I didn't want to get sick. But if I was in Thailand, I was going to eat the street food—especially when I saw a man standing over a wok under the sun making nothing but pad Thai. His tiny station was decked with a large bottle of fish sauce and bowls holding the various ingredients, which he threw into the wok with practiced speed. Shallots, tamarind paste, palm sugar, shrimp, garlic, tofu, scrambled eggs, rice noodles, bean sprouts. They all danced under the tongs in his hand as the dish came together before being heaped onto a paper plate, then dressed with chopped peanuts and a wedge of lime—every steaming, fragrant bit of it for about a dollar.

The scene reminded me of Brother Carl Shonk, my high school English teacher who was a monk. Brother Carl taught us about the *Canterbury Tales*, my favorite story being about the cook. The cook, Brother Carl told us ominously, would kneel beside his stew as he stirred it. Over time, he would develop a boil on his knee, which the cook would then squeeze into the stew to give it its signature flavor. I tried not to think of this as I stood on the corner devouring the best pad Thai I'd ever had.

Much as I wanted to continue on my own for the rest of the trip, I'd paid for the group tour and needed to make the most of what ensued, including being herded onto vans to Chiang Mai and back to Bangkok—a nine-hour drive each way.

"You have 15 minutes to look around the temple and take pictures!" was the usual directive from our chipper tour guide.

I happily waved goodbye to the group on that last day before catching the 12-hour sleeper train to Surat Thani—the last stop on the mainland. To get to the islands, you take a vomit-inducing ferry. It's not the rocking and rolling that gets you—it's the sound of your fellow passengers barfing into paper bags. All it takes is one, and before you know it, you're next in the retching chorus.

"Are you ready for something different?" beckoned the brochure for The Sanctuary in Koh Phangan, an island in southeast Thailand.

They say that when you find The One, you just know.

And that's exactly what happened when I flipped through the *Lonely Planet Thailand* guidebook and landed on a page about The Sanctuary in Koh Phangan. Branded an "alternative island resort," the place is impossibly difficult to reach—accessible only by speedboat or a precarious dirt road. This, of course, only adds to the allure.

There was no advance booking, so I opted to play it safe and stay at a luxury hotel on a nearby island. But on that first night, having a grand meal all by myself in the swank honeymoon resort, I knew this was not for me.

I decided to check out early and wing it.

When I finally arrived at The Sanctuary, via jeep on that newly built dirt road, I made a beeline for the legendary restaurant and its thick menu with page after page of vegetarian and seafood dishes. The open-air space is the centerpiece of a tropical paradise in every sense of the word. There are hammocks all around, massages whenever you want, and fruit as sweet as candy. I never wanted to leave this place, and, indeed, I ended up staying another week. This kind of flexibility is why I went freelance, after all, and I knew the work would be there when I returned.

A few of the staff were Westerners who'd gone a step further—they never went back home. I could see why, even though my little beach hut had no hot water, and my roommates were huntsman spiders the size of my hand clinging to the bamboo walls. There would be a half-dozen of them. You might think they were decals—until they started moving.

Taking a shower was like playing dodgeball: I'd zig-zag in and out of the cold water while simultaneously trying to splash the spiders before finally dousing them with a bucketful of water from the toilet. That was before the girl at the juice bar challenged me to make peace with them by recognizing that this was their home before it was ours.

There was a real community feel at The Sanctuary, especially at night. I couldn't be alone if I tried, and I started hanging out with three British girls who'd traveled together—a yoga teacher, a Pilates instructor, and a school principal. Then there was Mark, the Reiki master from Manchester, and John, an Australian who always wore Speedos.

And The Photographer.

He was from Belgium. I'd had my eye on him since that heart-thumping jeep ride to The Sanctuary, when he was nonchalantly shooting pictures as I was crouched and fearing for my life.

Maybe I'd finally do it: a fling. I was in paradise, free to reinvent myself once again. And I'd zeroed in on my target. Yes, I told myself, I can do this.

———

Waking up under the canopy in my hut, there was nothing to think about. I would slip into my swimsuit and sarong, step into flip flops, swipe on lip gloss, and stroll over to the restaurant—dewy leaves squishing beneath my feet. There, I would order a bowl of oatmeal, banana, and ground flax seeds. I'd plop onto a cushion beside my new British sisters or find a new friend to share breakfast with.

I felt good in my skin, London was far, far away, and there was nothing to do but soak up the natural beauty. Surely this was a recipe for that no-strings romantic "fun" I'd never known how to do back home. Could changing my environment on the outside change me within?

The Photographer was incredibly elusive. Only mosquitoes appeared to want me. This was not right.

I decided to check out the main draw at The Sanctuary: the detox center. Just to have a quick look. There was no way I was fasting.

Padding barefoot up the wooden steps, I spied a couple drinking watermelon juice at the bar. Trying not to draw attention to myself, I casually looked over the chalkboard offering 3 1/2- and seven-day fasts. I could tell the couple was watching me, and soon I learned they were fasting veterans, coming here year after year. When they found out I write about food and am obsessed with it, they told me I absolutely have to do this.

"No use coming all the way here if you're not," said the woman. "And no better way to confront your attachments to food," added the man.

Then they told me about the colonics—and with such zeal that you'd think they were talking about being treated to a four-course dinner at a Michelin-starred restaurant. Colonics, as I would learn, are a more intense version of an enema to clean the colon.

To say I was skeptical is an understatement. But if I wasn't getting any romantic action, I'd might as well take the next logical step and give up food, too. I'd draw the line at going topless on the beach. Fasting or not, I'd keep my clothes on—at least in public.

I signed up for the shorter fast and was sent off with a bunch of literature in preparation. I read it all, but not before gorging myself on coconut ice cream shakes and cake from the dessert case as if these were my last few days on earth.

To my relief, I learned this would not be a total fast. You're putting something into your belly about every two hours, be it an infusion of psyllium husk and clay (something my gag reflex never got used to), mineral tablets, your choice of juice (coconut, apple, watermelon, or carrot), and an evening vegetable broth spiked with cayenne pepper. The group atmosphere was almost cult-like with people popping pills in synchrony.

I joined my fellow first-day fasters for a colonic demonstration given by Moon, the detox center's lively manager. Moon looked like he was in his 30s, but he could have been much older (fasting and colonics supposedly kept you young).

Yes, he was giving a demonstration; because—news to me—these colonics are self-administered. Once inside the little colonic hut, Moon stretched out on a board—fully clothed—and proceeded to give us a surprisingly discreet demo on how to do this, which involved inserting a plastic tube into your rectum.

Later that day came the moment of truth. I undressed from the waist down, double-checked the shaky lock on the hut door, and made myself as comfortable as possible on a wooden plank while "The Girl from Ipanema" pumped out of the speakers and a giant bag of diluted coffee flowed into my bowels. If that sentence seems long, imagine what 45 minutes of this felt like.

Probably the best parts of doing a group cleanse are the post-colonic conversations, especially the ones started by the men. As you can guess, they tend to be slightly more squeamish about the process, and the ones in our group dealt with it by conjuring up a steady stream of comic material. In short, all we talked about was poop—how much, what color, what size.

The buzzword was "mucoid plaque," a digestive byproduct considered the Holy Grail of colon cleansing. There were pictures of the stuff in the detox center, and it's not pretty. We all secretly hoped to pass the elusive monster, but by the end of our fasts not one of us had produced the trophy.

(A word of caution: Medical professionals have denied the existence of mucoid plaque and state that sticking coffee up your butt is not only unnecessary, but dangerous. While I lived to tell the tale, proceed at your own risk.)

To my own surprise, I went topless. And it felt great. I'd done something completely unlike me.

Granted, I went to the other beach just over the hill, where fewer people would see me. But still. Change was indeed possible! What else was coming my way?

Feeling triumphant, I put on my bikini top, gathered my towel, and climbed the steps back up to The Sanctuary. I headed for the juice bar, where, to my delight, I spotted The Photographer ordering coconut water. He seemed just a bit flirty. I tried to contain effervescent bubbles of excitement within me. I told myself that maybe he was just being friendly. It was probably a cultural thing again. Nothing to do with me. But he didn't seem to fancy anyone else, either. And this, I admit, made me feel better.

Once you get the hang of a colonic, it's a breeze and goes fairly quickly, although the point of it is to hold the fluid in as long as you can before expelling it. One of the guys in my group was a wedding singer from Liverpool, and he had us howling with laughter when he revealed he was able to hold the entire contents of the colonic bag before releasing it. A medical marvel? Moon said he was one of two people he'd met who possessed this special talent.

As the days went on, I was amazed by how light and alive I

felt. By the end of the fast, my skin cleared, I felt incredibly alert, and my little muffin top had disappeared. Of course, attributing these changes to the colonic, the fast, or both would be a little shortsighted. I'm sure the sunshine, serenity, and seawater also had something to do with it.

I had my celebratory break-fast meal and stayed at the restaurant until only The Photographer and I were left. He told me about his dream to shoot for *National Geographic*, and I nodded like a good supportive woman. Then I told him all about the scary spiders in my room and the dark, dark walk back to my bungalow that required a flashlight.

It felt like we were finally getting somewhere.

And then he actually said, "I'm going to bugger off."

This was much too much, and I actually laughed at my luck. My cheeks were warm from the sun, and other parts of me were heating up, too. But the only thing that would keep me awake that night was the sound of rain on the thatched roof over my hut.

I'd never met so many men into yoga and meditation, and who also regularly do drugs.

Enter T-Shirt Guy. He swam up to me at the beach while I was floating on my back.

If there was ever an icon for a bad boy, he was it. Welsh, ripped, and with lips so full I had to keep reminding myself to look away. And to top it off, he liked me. But he was bad, bad news. He talked about Ecstasy (didn't care for cocaine) and getting high as casually as one would describe having a choco-late-chip cookie.

T-Shirt Guy designed printed T-shirts. He was making so much money selling them that he was able to go on an extended holiday for the next few months.

When I told him that I'd never even smoked pot, he looked at me and said, "I suddenly have the urge to corrupt you."

Later that night, I saw him at the Half Moon party, an outdoor rave held twice a month featuring techno, house, and urban music. He offered me a smoke; I declined. And I knew that if I'd offered him something else, he'd have gladly accepted. But I didn't, and I slinked back to my hut with flashlight in hand and a symphony of crackling, buzzing, eerily rustling noises all around me.

A lively chorus shook me out of my fitful sleep every morning in the hut. Birds. I could make out a duet between two of them. I slipped through the sheer canopy enveloping my bed and put on my uniform for the day: a bikini and the flowing fisherman's pants I'd bought on the beach for next to nothing.

Sipping on freshly pressed apple juice at the restaurant, I noticed the chalkboard next to the dessert case—which I was now avoiding without a problem. The board advertised the day's holistic events: yoga, meditation, shamanic trances. And that's how I found myself lying on my back above the rainforest, trying to find my power animal and trying even harder not to laugh.

I'd never done anything remotely shamanic—heavens, no. The Catholic schoolgirl in my head severely objected as I climbed the rocky path from the beach up to the yoga hall, a mosquito net-tented haven within earshot of the sea.

It was sunset, and the room was already dark. A few candles were lit. I recognized several faces in the dim glow.

We sat in a circle, all eyes cast on the shaman. With dark blond hair that fell below his muscled shoulders and an enviable toffee tan, Vinod looked like he should be on the cover of a romance novel. After a brief introduction, he told us to lie down in a circle, feet pointing toward the center. Within a few moments of silence, he began chanting in a sound I'd never heard from a human—dark, deep, and a little disturbing. He started to pound his drum rhythmically and purposefully. As he paced around the room, I heard it sweeping over me and back again, like a wave.

Vinod instructed us to picture a location in nature, and I immediately envision myself on a tropical beach. Still using my imagination, I was told to walk around for a while until I came to a hole big enough for me to fit into that leads to the underworld. This sounded scary. Nonetheless, I played along, watching my bare feet come to a halt upon spotting an opening in the pale sand.

I creep inside and start my descent, encouraged by Vinod's incessant drumming and calls to go deeper. I seem to be going down for ages. Finally, we reach the underworld. I picture an inhospitable cave crawling with spiders. Hell. I want to get out as soon as possible, so I plunge into the bottom of the ocean. Blue. I relax. Dolphins circle me and seem to smile. I'm supposed to be looking for my power animal, but something tells me it's not a dolphin. Then a turtle swims up close and plays a cheeky game of hide and seek.

"Don't forget to find your power animal!" roars Vinod, so I open my arms wide to encircle the turtle. It spins me around playfully.

Now we're told to dance like our animal if we want to, and this is where that prim and proper schoolgirl resurfaces. I can't take this seriously. I sneak a peek at the others around me and giggle at their serpent-like wriggling on the floor.

The drumming speeds up. Vinod tells us to head back up the hole without letting go of our new (or is it old?) friend and come into the room. I'm convinced I've concocted the turtle out of thin air, but I'm curious enough to look up what it might mean. Once back on WiFi, I learned that in shamanism, the turtle represents self-reliance, tenacity, and navigation skills. I like to think it symbolizes that wherever I go, I always carry my home.

When I told Vinod days later that I kept having nightmares after his trance session, he said, "Fantastic!" and advised me to invite my turtle to come to bed with me. Not exactly what I had in mind for a holiday fling.

The next day at lunch, I found out that The Photographer and the Pilates instructor spent the night together. I studied her expressions and words as if I were an anthropologist investigating another culture. She had this glow about her, but also a serene contentedness that was utterly foreign to me. She didn't seem the least bit anxious about what would happen next with this guy, or whether there would be anything next at all. She was completely unattached.

Would I ever truly cultivate this carefree quality myself?

On the flight home, I tried to pinpoint what exactly was so wonderful about my time at The Sanctuary, despite my zero score when it came to romance.

And I got it: that beach unleashed my femininity.

I wanted to wear flowing clothes and be near the water and feel the sun on my skin and be free and eat food that was good for me. I wanted to be in the moment, whatever the moment brought.

But it was winter on the other side of the world, and I was going back to a very different island.

BLISSED-OUT SALAD
Makes one large serving

I ate a huge salad very much like this nearly every non-fasting day at The Sanctuary. If I concentrate on the flavors, I can almost feel the sand between my toes.

1 tablespoon flax oil
1 teaspoon balsamic vinegar
1 garlic clove, pressed
½-inch piece of ginger, grated
2 handfuls baby greens
4-inch cucumber portion, halved and thinly sliced
1 rib celery, thinly sliced
1 tart apple (like Granny Smith), cored and thinly sliced
Handful cherry tomatoes, halved
2 tablespoons green onions, sliced
2 tablespoons dried, no-sugar added cranberries
Handful mixed sprouts
Handful cashews, chopped
Handful pecans, chopped
2 tablespoons sunflower seeds
A few sprigs fresh mint, torn
Black pepper

Whisk the oil, vinegar, garlic, and ginger together and toss with remaining ingredients, finishing with generous grindings of the black pepper.

MADE TO ORDER

The last time a man chased me down the street, he took off with my bag. My friend Grace, however, had a man run after her and ask her for a date. She told me the story at the Lazy Daisy Café in Notting Hill.

"I was walking home wondering why I'm still single when this John Lewis delivery guy stopped me, held my hand, and asked me out."

Now if only all you had to do was call ahead for a guy to be sent to your doorstep. I put down my forkful of broccoli and feta quiche. It looked like it had been nuked in the microwave, the natural bright green of the vegetable desaturated to a greyish gunk. I begged her to tell me more.

"Well, I asked him if he normally holds random women's hands on the street."

I peered down at the lackluster assortment of canned beans they'd thrown together with red-pepper flakes and called a salad.

"And he said no, that I was amazing. That he had to take me to dinner. He looked at my left hand and said that if I was married, he'd be a gentleman and leave, but that he couldn't let me go without trying."

It's easy to see why Grace stops traffic. She's 5'9 and British of Jamaican descent. She's gorgeous, can easily get away with subtracting ten years from her age, and always looks like she lives in a fashion photo shoot, which is a little annoying when we're at something called the Lazy Daisy Café, and I'm in my standard can't-cope-with-the-weather turtleneck, skinny jeans, furry boots, and bike-helmet hair.

Grace was a graphic designer at my old New York ad agency, and we immediately connected over our shared love of self-help books. We spoke the same language of affirmations, manifestation, and divine intervention.

Today we were talking about cosmic ordering, aka "The Secret," aka the law of attraction. Same thing, different spin. Grace put out a simple enough directive to the universe: I want to meet someone. And the universe delivered swiftly, in brilliant comedic fashion.

Grace rejected the doting deliveryman, even though she admitted—more than twice—that he was quite good-looking. Why did she say no? Because he didn't really fit with her idea of how her dream man would show up. The other thing to remember about this cosmic-ordering business:

Focus on what you want, but leave the "how" to the powers that be. Otherwise you turn intention into control, and trying to meddle with Mother Nature always messes things up.

Bottom line: be specific about what you want; you'll probably get exactly what you ask for. Now that's service.

In Thailand, I tried to script and direct the story. I attempted to maneuver The Photographer as if he were a character in my plot. I was trying to be the divine doing the intervening. And what if, in focusing my invisible camera lens on that one man, I completely missed a wider picture—with perhaps a more suitable prospect waiting in the wings?

————

You really should be careful what you wish for. Having sworn off online dating, I was nonetheless compelled to try again when I heard my friend Jennifer's story.

"I'm going to be alone for the rest of my life!" she sobbed into the phone.

Jen had just been dumped by yet another guy. I had never heard anyone in such despair, and I felt helpless to comfort her. Yet amazingly, she was depressed for all of one week and then decided to put herself on a certain dating site that asks you to answer as many questions as the SAT.

A successful lawyer in California, she resolved to give her love life as much attention as she did her career. Within two weeks, Jen had a date every night and was having the time of her life. Two months later, she was seriously involved with a man she thought she could marry. When it didn't work out, she found another guy she clicked with immediately. Within seven months of joining the site, Jen was pregnant and married. I couldn't believe it.

It was frustrating to me that, like Jen, I had been able to accomplish practically anything I put my mind to—moving to a foreign country with no job and no apartment and making it work, running the London Marathon with shin splints, learning to "speak British," traveling alone on the other side of the world —yet I couldn't seem to make this part of my life happen. The idea that I could take control of my love life like Jen made me feel hopeful, and it just so happened that the site she used to meet her husband had recently expanded to the UK.

I sat down for the long exercise with a cup of tea and a

couple of flapjacks. Nearly two hours later, I was presented with my matches and saw that most of them were US military men overseas. I never really thought of myself as a military wife, but when a thoughtful sailor stationed in Naples sent me a poetic message, I was swept away with the tide.

The Sailor was everything I thought I was looking for. He was educated, well-traveled, close to his family, liked to cook, and wrote exceptionally well-written accounts to me of his days at sea. Our correspondence and phone conversations were so easy that he made arrangements to visit London one weekend. I was apprehensive. Would our online chemistry translate to the real world? Would I have to spend all my time with him if it didn't? I re-watched *An Officer and A Gentleman* and started to get excited.

Turns out that the site was so darn good at matching me with someone compatible that this man could have been my long-lost twin brother. I showed him around town both Saturday and Sunday, waiting for some flutter in my heart. I wanted so badly to feel chemistry for him, and I felt comfortable enough to tell him this as we had afternoon tea a few hours before he flew home. The Sailor was disappointed and talked about how the women he had had a fiery start with were the very relationships that soon went down in flames. He observed how compatible we were and that this could very well be a slow burn. I knew he was right. The people I had initially experienced that untamable fire with—namely The Secret Agent—had ultimately burned me.

Had The Sailor been a Londoner—someone I could get to know on a casual basis—I might have let him drop anchor. Ultimately, I decided that I had to let this one drift away.

Then I was matched with The Pilot.

The Pilot talked of his love for his brothers in the Air Force and left me an adorable voice message before our first date asking what he could bring me from the base.

"Twix, Oreos, Pillsbury Mix, Reese's Pieces, whaddya want?"

It was all the sweeter given he was taking me to The Ivy, a London legend dating to 1917. I had really only suggested it as a joke, but The Pilot was eager to please. I tried to dissuade him from the idea, worried that it was a bit too much for a first meeting, but he insisted, saying it "sounded awesome" and wanted to check it out.

This time, my anxiety about the bill was as acute as ever. If The Sailor was my long-lost twin, The Pilot—eight years younger than me—was my little brother. I declined his suggestion of an appetizer and went straight to the salmon fishcake with spinach and sorrel sauce—the cheapest thing on the menu. I also offered to split a beautiful dessert of seasonal berries—frozen so they looked like they were preserved in an unseasonable frost. The age gap didn't seem to bother The Pilot one bit; and he told me, to my astonishment, that he couldn't wait to get married and settle down. I had to break the news to a uniformed man again: I wasn't ready to enlist.

But I had to ask myself why. Was this guy truly not a good match, or was I still subconsciously committed to pushing away what I wanted? And if I *was* pushing it away, did I really want it to begin with?

I quit online dating once more. It seemed like the universe was screaming that I still needed to get to know someone else a little better.

Me.

DRINKING IT UP

I STARTED READING *The Power of Now*, keeping a gratitude journal, getting up early to do yoga, meditating by candlelight, and really trying to find my happiness within. I also volunteered to serve on the rowing club's committee, which included doling out Pimm's during the Oxford and Cambridge boat race. Every spring, crews from both universities compete on a 4.2-mile stretch of the Thames in west London. It's a big party for onlookers lining the river. Pimm's, the drink of choice for the day, is a gin-based liquor mixed with lemonade, cucumbers, strawberries, oranges, and mint. Meanwhile, my food blog led to some TV appearances and a series of articles in *Men's Health* magazine, including a how-to piece on who fires up the best barbecue: Americans, Australians, or South Africans. Answer: they all do it differently.

I was convinced I had now really and truly "arrived" and that life had even bigger and better things in store for me.

And so it was. Because that's when I met The Supersize, an ex-rower.

Standing 6'5, he played rugby every weekend and could drink for the entire team. He was enormously proud of his body, and the tales of him dancing atop tables wearing backless chaps were legend. There was even a YouTube video to prove it.

On our first date, The Supersize drank 16 pints of beer—I counted. But I made excuses for it and pretended it didn't bother me; after all, the date had gone from brunch to past dinner, and I had to get with the *programme*.

He seemed to hold the alcohol well—too well. And he was so attentive! As we trained and bussed from one pub to another, he was so excited about me that at one point he looked up at the sky while holding my hand and yelled, "Winning!"

At the end of the night, he walked me to the bus stop and slurred, "So, Jess, this is what I do every Saturday. I go to the pub with my friends, and I drink. Are you OK with that?"

Completely overcome by finally being on a date with someone I wanted to jump—even if I needed a trampoline—I chirped, "Of course, we all like different things!"

Then he added two more questions: did I have any cats, and was I bisexual?

No to both, I said.

"Good," he replied with relief. "Because I dated a bisexual lady once, and they always go with the girl."

I never asked about the cat.

The next day, he called. Yes, an actual phone call.

"Jess, I want you to know I'm not usually *that* crazy."

Great, now we were both lying.

It was an opposites-attract match in the truest sense, and we both forged ahead knowing full well it was doomed. I reveled in the sheer size of him, while he felt even larger next to me. He would give me piggyback rides down the seven flights of stairs from my flat and swing me over his head à la *Dirty Dancing* for anyone who would watch. When we took a bubble bath together—his back against my chest—it was like playing the cello. When I'd set the table, he joked I should use plastic so his footsteps wouldn't shatter the glassware. In a wave of early-dating zeal, he even suggested we visit his mother in the country sometime. I was ecstatic.

Everything was fun, until it wasn't. I was as much a fish out of water with him as he drank like one. A barracuda.

One day in his car, he suddenly became serious.

"There's something I want to mention. We've been dating for over a month, and if there's anything at all you're upset about, I want to know. I don't want surprises."

It turned out that his last girlfriend had broken up with him after a few seemingly good weeks, and he didn't want to go through that again. I was touched by his vulnerability, and I kept trying to silence the voice within me that said yes, I was concerned about something.

But when we celebrated his 30th birthday and I watched the bartender try to dissuade him from yet another beer, I couldn't hold it in any longer. The next morning, over scrambled eggs and focaccia at Carluccio's, I finally brought up the issue. It was right after he told me "all my money goes to alcohol," and of course it was his way of waving the flag so I could escape before it was too late for both of us.

I took the bait. I confessed that his drinking worried me, and that I felt terrible watching someone as fit and full of life change the way he did when he drank. I tried to boost his ego as I carefully laid out my case, but as we walked past the pond in Hyde Park, I felt his hand go limp in mine. There it was again—*the shift*: that awful, gut-turning feeling when you know the person you're dating has had a change of heart, and not for the better. That night, we slept on opposite sides of the bed.

He began acting indifferent to me, and he invited his flat mate—a woman who clearly had a crush on him—along to our weekend in the country. That's it, I thought—it's over. I convinced myself that I never should have brought up the issue, that I should have accepted him as he was. Was I just being judgmental?

Filled with self-doubt, I asked him to come over so I could clear the air. I told him I felt I had made a big deal out of nothing, and that I simply wasn't used to drinking much. To my surprise, he took me to meet his mother—just the two of us. 6-feet tall, she was very sweet and thought I was the cutest thing. But when she tried to refill my wine glass, The Supersize quickly barked, "Mum, she's not like you!"

I wouldn't admit it to myself, not yet: no amount of effort could keep this relationship afloat.

———

The only way I've ever been able to relate to alcoholics and smokers is via sugar. I know it's not good for me, and I'm getting better at cutting back, but I still do it. So when the news broke that they were going to put disease graphics on cigarette packs, I instantly knew it wouldn't work. It would be like slapping obesity images on chocolate bars. I'd still eat them. Wouldn't you?

Trying to distract myself from the impending breakup with The Supersize, I signed up for a yoga teacher training workshop in Soho. For three days I was immersed in the philosophy of acceptance and appreciation versus attachment and aversion. What did I do at lunchtime? Head straight over to Ladurée in Piccadilly. Once there, I asked if they happened to sell their hot-chocolate mix. "Well," said the girl, "You can buy this cocoa powder here, but we also have the hot chocolate to go."

What?

You mean the almost-molten-chocolate-bar-that-clings-to-the-inside-of-the-cup hot chocolate, in a paper cup? Something so precious, downgraded like that?

Yes. Seemingly compelled, I said yes. I paid for my cup, then I perched on the steps outside the Royal Academy, taking in each mouthful slowly, as if drag by drag.

A week later, The Supersize broke up with me over the phone. He mumbled something about being under too much stress at work and not having enough time for a relationship.

"Can't we work it out?" I asked.

"No," he insisted. "Besides, you don't have a TV."

I didn't, and to this day, that remains the best breakup excuse I've ever heard. The absurdity of it helped to soften the blow.

———

I never intended not to get a television. It all started when I moved out of Rosie's flat into a place of my own. I became acutely aware of the lack of TV when I sat down to dinner my first night there. Suddenly, without the usual background noise, I realized how I was now focusing my attention fully on the food in front of me. My dinner became an event, unlike the usual mindless eating I was doing before.

Even so, I still thought I'd get around to getting a TV. But as the days went on, I wasn't really missing it. Then the letters started coming.

If you don't live in the UK, you might be surprised to hear that you need a license to watch television, and that there's a crackdown team in place should you think you can get away without buying a license. The letters start out quite friendly, then build up into paranoia-inducing missives:

"Most people who claim not to have a television actually do." At this point, it almost became a mission to stay without a TV and prove it.

The no-TV thing was a useful barometer when it came to

guys. "Brilliant!" was a good sign. "That's weird" meant I should probably change the channel.

BIGGER-PICTURE PUMPKIN MUFFINS
Makes a dozen

No TV gave me a whole lot more time in the kitchen, especially when I was missing home and all the flavors that reminded me of it—like pumpkin during the fall.

I think the popularity of muffins and cupcakes lies in their ability to satisfy the childhood urge to have a whole cake all to oneself while pleasing the grown-up sensibility of portion control. They're the one instance where not sharing can be a very respectable thing indeed.

> 1 cup (120 g) all-purpose flour (plain flour in the UK)
> ½ cup (60 g) spelt flour
> 1 teaspoon baking powder
> 15 oz can solid-pack pumpkin
> 1/3 cup (76 g) butter, melted
> 2 large eggs
> ½ teaspoon cinnamon
> ¼ teaspoon ground ginger
> ¼ teaspoon ground nutmeg
> 1 cup (200 g) sugar
> ¼ cup (50 g) light brown sugar
> ½ teaspoon baking soda
> ½ teaspoon sea salt

1. Put oven rack in middle position and preheat oven to 350°F (180°C). Tuck liners into muffin cups.
2. Combine flours and baking powder in a small bowl.

3. Whisk together pumpkin, butter, eggs, spices, sugars, baking soda, and salt in a large bowl until smooth, then whisk in flour mixture until just combined.

4. Divide batter among muffin cups (I use an ice-cream scoop). Each cup should be about three-quarters full.

5. Bake until puffed and golden brown, about 25-30 minutes. If a knife inserted into one of the muffins comes out clean, they're done.

6. Cool in pan on a rack five minutes, then transfer muffins from pan to a wire rack. Tear into one while still warm.

IN DUE COURSES

You DON'T PLANT a seed and dig it up the next day to see why it hasn't sprouted. There's an innate intelligence that makes it happen. Yet we ignore this in our lives, pushing and prodding so that we stunt things before they have a chance to bloom. Why does our species believe we are beyond the laws of the very nature we are inextricably a part of? Patience is not merely a virtue; it's vital.

At a dinner in Chinatown with my rowing buddies, the conversation turned toward meeting "the one." When you're looking for love, the idea of a single perfect match feels both encouraging and defeating. It only takes one. That's what makes it at once so precious, so elusive, so easy, so hard.

Chili soft-shell crab is served. I zone out for a bit. The breading is airy and sea-salty; the crab pulls apart without resistance. In one mouthful my mind fills with memories of both southern Thailand and Tomoe Sushi in New York—the only place I've ever waited two hours for a table.

Meanwhile, my friends continued to ponder the seemingly random nature of finding a partner.

"It's all about timing," said Dennis, my fellow Miami native.

The crab breading was all that was left. Chopsticks in hand, I chased what remained around the plate. "Yeah, you can meet the right person at the wrong time," added another rower.

Pause. I'm not sure about that. In my mind, there is no wrong time. Life gives you exactly what you need when you need it. Every moment is the right time. If not, it's not the right person. And even that's not entirely accurate, because "the wrong" person was still exactly right for you at that time in your journey.

I've read that soulmates are the people who come into our lives to mirror what needs changing, and the connection is so intense it's naturally short-lived. Both the relationship and the breakup feel like pulling teeth—it's your old self making way for the new, and then there's more pain when the new teeth come in.

———

Oh, the lessons. How mercilessly yet lovingly they come. Heartbreaking, bittersweet, utterly necessary.

I'm in central London tasting the hot chocolate at Paul, the French boulangerie chain, for the second time in a week. This time I've gone for the large. That's the kind of impression it made.

The skin has already started to set and pucker. Check. It's thin enough to drink, thick enough to spoon. Check. It hugs the inside of the cup as it does the back of my throat. Check. It tastes deeply of chocolate with a light touch of *je ne sais quoi*. Check.

As I tip the cup one final time to taste the last drop, I wonder what the recipe might be and whether I could get it. Then my heart sinks as I think: copious cream, unscrupulous sugar. But then it dawns on me: the sum of this hot chocolate would never be so wonderful were it not for all its parts, the sinful as well as the seductive.

When The Boyfriend and I started dating, people told me that I was too young and inexperienced to know whether I was truly in love. They said that when I got older, I'd know better. But the opposite became true. The more time passed, the more I realized that *was* love. The relationship might not have been meant to last forever, but it was love nonetheless. To have expected the pain to vanish quickly was the real fantasy.

I'd read that true love comes in three stages. First, there is love without knowledge. This is when we project our fantasies onto someone we barely know, thus creating that initial giddiness. Then comes knowledge without love. Here is where we find out that the projection screen is human, one who has been brought into our lives to mirror back to us what we secretly don't like about ourselves, and vice versa. Initial attraction is actually nature's clever trick to get us to this second stage so that we come face to face with ourselves via another, deal with our demons, and grow.

Sticking it out at this stage is like boiling maple sap into syrup: it bubbles up a lot of friction, but the rewards are ultimately sweeter than what you started with. It only happens when we trust in the process and give each other the unconditional acceptance we want for ourselves. It's all too easy to bail at this point, but then you miss the third stage and the icing on the cake: love with knowledge. In other words, ignorance is lust. It's acceptance—loving what is—that's bliss.

Covent Garden reminded me too much of The Supersize—that's where we'd had our first date, so I broke up with it, too. I reluctantly parted with my favorite lunch spots without so much as a goodbye.

I was conflicted.

Would the Brazilian waitress at Hazuki wonder if I had grown tired of my usual sea-salted mackerel and bottomless cups of green tea?

"Maybe it just wasn't exciting enough for her," she'd worry, as she dashed between the lower and upper floors with trays of tempura and spreads of silken sashimi.

I could picture the overzealous Philippine and Italian waiters at my Indian standby, Masala Zone, looking glumly out the windows for my small self, thinking perhaps they had heaped on the charm—and the chapatis—a bit too much.

Or maybe the busy, well-traveled cooks at Wild Food Café, witnessing yet another week go by without my patronage, would finally take chalk to board and slash those filet mignon prices from their mini falafels. And would it finally be time for Food for Thought to ponder giving me some oxygen in its cramped dining room?

Would the talented bakers behind Kastner and Ovens think their addictive cakes put me over the glycemic edge—I mean index—propelling me to seek refuge in the arms of something more (blood-sugar) stabilizing?

I highly doubted it, and they'd be wasting their time if they did. How many times have we, after being dumped, agonized over what could have driven our love away? We replay scenarios to pinpoint the exact axis of interaction that made our beloved decide they just weren't into us. And if you are the dumper, what goes around usually comes right back at you.

There is a particular species of monkey that can be trapped and captured quite easily. All you have to do is take a box and carve a hole in it just big enough for the monkey to put its hand through. You drop a nut into the hole and wait for the monkey to grab it. When it tries to pull its hand out, guess what? It can't. Gripping the nut, the monkey tries and tries to release itself from the trap. What's the one thing it needs to do? Drop the nut. But it won't, because at that moment the monkey acts like that is the only nut in the world. It's willing to forsake a whole future of nuts for that one inside the box.

That was me after every break up. I was that monkey.

Here I was again, shortsighted and stuck. But I had to snap out of it, and quickly.

Because there was a wedding to go to.

My Serpentine friend Nicola was getting married in Granada. It was a two-day affair on a glorious fall weekend, with a party Saturday and the wedding Sunday.

I arrived on Friday and wandered around looking for a place to have dinner. Even though I'm fluent in the language, I found it more difficult being by myself in Spain than I did in Thailand. Every restaurant I passed was filled with groups of people happily eating together. If the Spanish tourism authority hired me to write its English tagline, it would be easy: "Spain is for Sharing."

As I sat down to a heaping plate of calamari and the joyful sounds that reminded me of my *familia*, I longed to have them share this with me.

One of our family favorites is *churros con chocolate*, and it just so happens I was staying in an area well known for them. *Churros*, for the sadly uninitiated, are fat pieces of fried dough, served alongside ridiculously thick hot chocolate. It's more like pudding. The French have nothing on this.

My search began at breakfast the next morning, conveniently right outside my hotel at an outdoor café. A huge bunch of *churros* accompanied a comparatively small mug of the rich liquid chocolate. The spoon resting alongside it wasn't for adding sugar. This chocolate was too thick too drink. But as I dipped the *churros* into it, I closed my eyes and convinced myself that this was, indeed, what I was looking for: the ultimate hot chocolate, and right by the hotel! I left satisfied, believing this was it—no other chocolate would do.

That afternoon, it was time for the pre-wedding party, held at the vacation home Nicola and her fiancé Peter had bought a year before on one of their trips. They had been scooting around Granada on Peter's motorbike when they spotted the house and fell in love with it. To me, this was a fairytale love story—a real one. No drama. The party was held on the wraparound terrace overlooking the town. For hours, we drank sangria and feasted on Spanish delicacies.

The next morning—or nearly noon, if I'm honest—I stepped into the Spanish sunshine and went straight for the convenient café. Then I had a hunch to keep going. I walked around the plaza. No sign of *churros con chocolate*. I walked a bit more and eyed what other places were serving. Nope. "I guess that café was it after all," I thought. But then I walked a bit further, ignoring the rumblings in my belly.

I rounded a corner and spotted a friendly, busy place with an empty table by the door and a sign saying they did half portions of churros. I ordered mine with the required cup of you know what, and when I looked down at it, I knew. Even before I lifted it to my lips, I knew. Thick enough to dip, thin enough to drink. And a plate of churros just my size. Oh, the joys I would have missed had I settled for that other café! It took me a couple of times around the block, but I had found it.

The other tagline contender: "Spain is for Soul Searching."

That afternoon, it was time for the church wedding and reception. On the heels of my latest breakup, the wedding filled me with both hope and hopelessness. Surrounded by friends and the beauty of the landscape, I tried to remember that my life was so much bigger than the one thing I hadn't gotten "right."

Isla had indeed wound up with her perfect guy, almost a year to the day I had suggested she put him out of her mind. My prediction that they would be together had come true. The Barrister was there, too—still single and still not making any moves in my direction, despite sitting next to me during the ceremony, dancing together at the reception, and going for hot chocolate the next morning at my new favorite place. This was a friendship, and no more. By this point, I wasn't expecting anything else. Witnessing Nicola's happiness that weekend confirmed that I did want more ... with someone who truly wanted me. But was that sort of love story reserved for other people?

FED UP TO WELL FED

EVERY WEEK, St. James Church in Piccadilly hosts talks by Alternatives, a forum for speakers from the personal growth and well-being fields. All the notable self-help superstars held events there, and I had become an audience regular.

The latest guest was a Native American healer who stood at the front of the church, holding a single eagle feather as he spoke movingly about how we have lost our connection to the earth while at the same time attempting to control it.

He talked of his nature tours in Arizona and being dumbfounded by people who'd point to a tree and ask, "What kind of tree is that?" His answer: "Tree."

His love of simplicity and respect for the natural flow of life hit a nerve. When the talk was over, I stayed behind to meet him.

As my turn approached, I wasn't sure what I was going to tell this man. But as I stepped forward, tears came quickly—and so did my question.

"Do you believe in soulmates?" I asked. "Because I'm having a really hard time finding mine."

Here I was in front of another ponytailed man—a decade

after my meeting with the priest—hoping he would have the answer I needed.

But this guy was not letting me off so easily.

He smiled.

"You know what I call that?" came the reply. "Control."

Then he told me to surrender—*really* surrender.

He placed his palm on my forehead.

"Get out of this place," he said.

Then he moved his hand over my heart.

"And start living from here."

Just how the heck was I supposed to do that? Was I supposed to just know? I clearly didn't. Was there a school for living from the heart? I needed step-by-step instructions.

But I didn't ask the healer any of this. There were others waiting in line behind me.

Before I knew it, I was down the rabbit hole again. It was approaching Christmas, and all the progress I made after The Secret Agent seemed to have disappeared.

It was a perfect storm: the credit crunch of 2008 that dried up all my freelance work, my 34th birthday, and yet another breakup. The relationship had been a short one, but it was long enough for me to start attaching to it all the hopes and dreams that come when you finally "meet someone." Suddenly, the fact that I had been living in the UK for nearly five years and was once again single drove me into a depression I couldn't shake. I was dismayed, wishing I could peel off my body—my being—and step into someone else's life.

In New York, we go to the shrink; in London, you go to the pub. At a loss, I headed for the library. Bingeing on more self-help books, I kept stumbling across something called the Hoffman Process.

The eight-day residential retreat was supposed to help you break free from the past and create the future you want—all for double my monthly rent payment. I had read it was a transformational experience on par with a year's worth of therapy. It's intense: you're not allowed contact with the outside world while you're there (no phones, no laptops, and even books are surrendered when you check in). Cult alarm bells went off in my head, but after hours of research, I had not come across anything sinister.

The thought of parting with the money pained me, but the prospect of crying on the couch any longer was unbearable. In the midst of the fog, I could see that I had understood all the personal-growth concepts intellectually, but I had failed to integrate them long term. I needed something that would stick, and Hoffman was based on experiential techniques aimed at breaking the negative patterns we adopted as children in an attempt to secure a parent's love. I was intrigued. Could an eight-day retreat give me the lasting change I was after? The testimonials seemed too good to be true, but the headline on the Hoffman website summed up exactly what I'd been feeling: "When You're Fed Up with Being Fed Up."

After thinking about it for a week, I signed up. I knew one thing: I couldn't continue as I was. Drastic measures were in order.

On the appointed day, I took the No. 10 bus outside my apartment building to King's Cross station, where I boarded a train to Kent. The Process would take place at Oxon Hoath, a lavish 14th-century estate in the peaceful countryside about 45 minutes outside London. When I arrived at registration, my luggage was almost as heavy as my heart. Along with 16 other participants and three teachers, this would be my home, hell, and hopefully heaven for the next eight days. I quipped to the girl with whom I had shared a cab that the Hoffman Process already felt like a cross between being in a Jane Austen adaptation and a reality show. I had high hopes, but I also had my guard up.

We weren't allowed to tell one another what we did for a living, creating a rare opportunity to interact without the labels we normally carry around. Stripped of our outer identities, we were just people going through a tough time for one reason or another, sharing a desperate need to make it all better. When the masks came off, our souls were laid bare. It was a lesson in the power of vulnerability—disclosing the darkest parts of ourselves actually opened us up to intimacy.

When they announced we'd be working from just after breakfast until well past dinner, I was worried that I'd get bored or burnt out. But every moment was structured in such a way that not only did I not have time to think about my failed romantic relationships, I was actually getting somewhere. A turning point for me and a testament to the power of group dynamics was this: even though the majority of participants had partners and children—what I thought I needed to be happy—they still had their personal demons to battle.

Through group and individual work, the first part of the week was spent releasing the anger associated with our negative patterns. I learned that I had suppressed anger toward my father, that as a child I couldn't make sense of his fragmented presence and had to pretend everything was OK. I had even convinced myself that it had made me a stronger, more independent person. Now I was being asked to vent every bit of pent-up rage from my childhood, both on paper and with a plastic baseball bat.

"Where did you put all the anger?" asked the Hoffman teacher.

I didn't know. I was raised to think anger was un-ladylike.

The teacher advised me to let it rip. I politely told him that I would not be using foul language, thank you very much. But when we got into a rhythm pounding cushions with our baseball bats, there was an unleashing of something primal, something from deep within. There was yelling, there was cursing, there was stomping—and it felt euphoric. I'd go to bed exhausted yet somehow lighter. A few days in, I started feeling good about being there. And the food—the food! Mostly local and seasonal, it was excellent.

After purging our past, it was time to make peace with it. Now my aching muscles gave way to puffy eyes as we were guided to find compassion for our parents by understanding how they too had been wounded as children. I realized that, in never allowing myself to grieve my father's disownment, every romantic breakup had triggered a mourning response. The more I forgave, accepted, and loved myself, the more I was able to do this for others, including my parents. This was also true for my fellow participants. Even though we were all doing the same exercises, they felt personalized, illustrating the universal nature of human experience.

I saw that without a man around the house and my mother still grieving his loss, I had grown up fast and coped by taking things into my own hands. The result? Control freak. This had served me well in many ways—I seemed to accomplish everything I set my mind to, except for one glaring thing: love. It was the one thing I couldn't control, and it drove me crazy.

My controlling pattern would be put to the test every hour of the Process. We had no clue what was coming next and were even blindfolded at times. To my surprise, I loved it. Letting go and letting someone else run the show was both liberating and fun—something I promised myself I'd remember in my next relationship.

I had gone from stuck to struck, and as departure time drew closer, I feared it would all slip through my fingers, especially as the next two days were to be spent in quiet reflection at home. Indeed, when I stepped out into the real world, I felt like the spaceship had landed. The city buzz felt so alien, so unnatural. And yet I was at peace, with a newfound appreciation for this place I had made my home. I didn't rush to check my messages, many of which were from concerned friends who were waiting to rescue me in case I had joined a cult.

When I texted them to say I was spending the weekend alone, their suspicions were aroused. But as soon as they saw me again, they were relieved, partly because I was finally talking about something other than the breakup. I was filled with renewed energy, that same fire in my belly that had propelled me from one side of the Atlantic to the other almost five years before. But most importantly, I felt fully present and more in touch than ever with the innate joy and peace that are always accessible to us. The breakup seemed light years away even though it had made up my entire world only eight days before.

I had a new way of looking at my short relationship with The Supersize. It would be easy to blame everything on his drinking, but that wasn't it. The problem was that I hadn't been honest—neither with him nor with me. From the beginning, he told me exactly what he liked to do—drink. I pretended it didn't matter. He may have had a drinking problem, but I had an honesty problem. Maybe, they were one and the same—just different human ways of coping with both the desire and the fear of being loved. My heart softened for him and me.

Toward the end of the Process, we were asked to look every other participant in the eye and tell them what we appreciated about them. After the exercise, we learned that the qualities we admired were also present in us—otherwise we wouldn't be able to see them. It works in reverse, too: that which we criticize in others is often present in ourselves. Since then, when-ever I make a judgement, I ask myself, "Wait, do *I* do that?" And if I admire someone, I wonder, "How can I step into more of that?"

On the first day of the Process, we were asked to reveal our heart's most fervent desire. Mine was to find lasting love. I did—for myself and with the light in everyone I met that week.

COMPASSION APPLESAUCE
Makes as much as you want

You can learn a lot about relationships by making applesauce. To start, find yourself some cooking apples, such as Bramley or Braeburn. You'll need about five or six for a big jar. It's OK if they are a little bruised; most things in life are when you meet them.

Next, wash and scrub the apples and get out your chopping board. Peel each apple carefully and slowly. Go too fast too soon and ... ouch! You might lose some of your apple, not to mention a lot of your finger.

Cut the peeled apples into quarters and core them. It doesn't matter which you do first; but again, don't rush this too much. Now cut them again into chunks and snuggle them inside a heavy saucepan. Squeeze the juice of half a lemon over them, put the lid on, and set the pan over low heat. That's it. Let it go to work. After about 10 minutes, just give things a little stir, then put the lid back on and enjoy the sweet scent filling your home.

After another 25 minutes, come back and lift the lid. Voila! Applesauce. You didn't need to mash it. You didn't need to prod it. You could, if you like, dunk a cinnamon stick in it if you want to spice things up. Actually, that's usually a good idea. But aren't you glad you didn't turn up the heat to speed things along? Look, it cooked. All by itself.

On the flip side, it's also surprisingly easy to not pay enough attention to your applesauce. It will try to let you know—bubbling up a fuss and making the lid go thwack. If you don't get back in the kitchen with it and take it off the heat, then before you know it, your applesauce has burned.

Somewhere between laissez-faire and micromanagement lies the perfect applesauce. Depends on the apples. Depends on you.

Sometimes you can save applesauce, and sometimes you can't. If the applesauce isn't completely burned and you started with good apples, it's worth trying to save it if you are willing to make the effort. Just leave the burned bit on the bottom and go to town thinking of creative ways to put the remaining applesauce to good use. If you can't, put a Band-Aid on that finger. If you happen to run into a nice new batch of apples, bring them home. Remember what went right before and what didn't. Roll up your sleeves again. Make some applesauce. Then savor it, slowly.

DESSERT

STIR WITH LOVE

"You and your flat stomach," said Isla as she hugged me.

We were at a garden party that inevitably turned into an everyone-crammed-in-the-kitchen gathering, thanks to a bitter blast of freezing rain. Why was I not used to this after more than five years in London? I should have known by now that a warm week in March on these shores is really just a wink from above, and that you shouldn't even think about taking the flannel sheets out of commission until at least May.

Isla's comment about my waist made me realize the transformative power of food and how you can, literally, reshape your body. When I came back from the Hoffman Process in late December feeling so much freer inside, I decided to start the new year with a monthlong detox. That meant no animal products, sugar, dairy, or gluten. After I made it through January, I wanted to see if I could make clean eating more of a permanent thing, so I kept dropping the processed foods and upping my intake of fresh veggies and fruit. My body was feeling the love. I wasn't just slimmer, I felt better in my skin.

Meanwhile, there had been another milestone. In honor of Valentine's Day, I decided to go to a "bring a mate" party—the premise being that you invite a friend of the opposite sex you aren't interested in. I chose The Barrister. This crush had been going on for years, and clearly it wasn't mutual. I wanted to set the record straight and show him there were no hard feelings.

And in a twist that seems perfectly orchestrated by a higher power with a sublime sense of humor, I wound up leading my long-standing crush right into the arms of love.

Because on the night of the party, he met his future wife.

After reading countless self-help books, I saw that they all generally say the same thing. Whether they're about finding love, moving on, leading a richer life, or discovering your purpose, it all comes down to two words: acceptance and gratitude. In other words, happiness comes from loving yourself and your circumstances exactly as they are—even if you want to change them. I would add this: laugh whenever possible.

On one bookstore browsing trip, I came across *The Surrendered Single* by Laura Doyle. Once I got over the title, I saw that the premise was once again the same: don't try to change him (acceptance) and focus on what you love about him rather than what ticks you off (gratitude). And there was another little nugget in there I warmed to: the idea that there is no perfect partner, rather an imperfect person who's perfect for you. Which, if you think about it, is just another way of saying the same thing: get over yourself and embrace what you've got, whether you're in love or singledom.

Perfect imperfection. I was thinking about this as I was making my favorite standby: the stir fry. There might be a few fundamentals in the preparation, yet my idea of a perfect stir fry is probably quite different from yours. Google "stir fry" and you get millions of results—and quite a discrepancy about whether there should be a hyphen. One thing is certain: stir frying, like romance, needs to be devoid of measurements. It's much more satisfying—even essential—to dispense with rigidity and just go with the flow. Just make sure you keep things moving—in this case, over high heat.

MY PERFECT STIR-FRY
Portions vary

This is the stir fry that does it for me. There's nothing fancy about it. It fills me up. It's good to my body. It's always dependable. It's nice to look at and even better to taste.

I've purposely left out quantities from this recipe, because the point is to use however much—or little—you want to eat. So it's perfect every time.

Brown rice noodles
Coconut oil
Carrots
Celery
Broccoli
Garlic clove
Fresh ginger
Mushrooms
Firm tofu
Light tahini
Tamari
Raw cashews
Toasted sesame seeds

1. Put a pot of water to boil and set a wok over high heat.
2. Cut the carrots into matchsticks, slice the celery, and add to the wok along with a little water.
3. While the vegetables steam, cut the broccoli into

small florets, rinse them and add to the wok, adding more water if necessary.

4. When the broccoli's green amps up (about a minute), transfer all the veggies to a plate.

5. Add some coconut oil to the wok, then mince the garlic and ginger and throw them in.

6. Place the noodles in the pot of the now-boiling water.

7. Clean and quarter the mushrooms, then add to the wok. Stir, stir, stir.

8. Slice the tofu and add it in, too. Sizzle, sizzle.

9. Meanwhile, mix one part tahini to four parts tamari in a small bowl.

10. Push the mushrooms and tofu up to the side of the wok and add a little more oil to the center.

11. Drain the noodles and add them to the oil, breaking them up with a long wooden fork.

12. Now add the vegetables back in along with the cashews, sauce, and sesame seeds. Keep stirring everything together vigorously for a few more seconds. Eat with gratitude.

DULCE DE LECHE BARS
12 squares

Dulce de Leche ("milk dessert") has become popular outside of the Hispanic culture, but growing up in a Cuban family meant we always had some around the house. This addictive recipe lets me enjoy that familiar treat without the usual dairy and sugar. Instead, it gets its rich sweetness from lucuma, a native Peruvian fruit with a heavenly maple taste known as the "gold of the Incas." It's also high in beta-carotene, niacin, and iron. *Salud*!

2 cups (200 g) almond meal from almond milk*
¼ cup (52 g) coconut oil
¼ cup (59 ml) agave
2 cups (350 g) pitted dates
1 cup (115 g) lucuma powder
1 vanilla bean, scraped
¼ teaspoon sea salt

1. Put everything (in the order listed) in a high-speed blender (such as a Vitamix) or food processor and blend until smooth. You will need to scrape the mixture down with a spatula until the dates are fully blended. The mixture will be very thick.
2. Spread into a 9 x 9 pan and place in the freezer for at least two hours.
3. Cut into squares. Eat straight from the freezer.

*Almond milk is easy to make. Just blend one part soaked almonds with three parts filtered water, then push through a fine-mesh sieve. For this recipe, you use the leftover "pulp" after you've strained the milk well.

SWEET SURRENDER

I'D AVOIDED its presence in my living room until I forgot it was there—The Secret Agent's cufflink. The last remnant of those feverish, then despairing, and ultimately transformative days. It had been two years since I had tucked the cufflink behind a framed photo of a friend's wedding, hoping the joyful memories captured in that picture would somehow sweeten the pain and confusion of yet another romance gone sour.

I was more than ready to let it go, so I took it down to the charity shop on Kensington High Street. The woman behind the counter brought it near her face to have a closer look, then placed it in her sorting pile. Where the solo cufflink would end up, I'd never know.

Not long after, I was freelancing at a digital marketing agency in Farringdon, happily heading to an Italian cafe for lunch, when I saw The Accountant walking straight toward me. Caught off guard, he froze and shoved his hands in his pockets. I had rejected his offer to meet, and this was awkward.

We exchanged pleasantries and walked our separate ways. Then suddenly I thought, "Hey, I know what he looks like under those clothes."

I laughed to myself, because I finally had the answer to the question that had driven me crazy all those years ago: how it's totally possible to get naked with someone and then move on. I wasn't sure if I should be comforted or dismayed by this revelation. But for me, it was some kind of progress.

In hindsight, I could also appreciate that The Accountant was a good guy. He had broken up with me in person (not something to be taken for granted these days), and he was clearly in distress when he did it.

I could, by now, also admit that when I asked him for a blood test, I was really testing how much he really wanted me. I wanted to feel special. Meanwhile, he was just a regular guy with a crush who was in over his head. And he was man enough to self-reflect, trying to make it up to me a year later.

I'll never know what would have happened if I had agreed to meet him again—if I had stepped onto the train when the sliding doors reopened. Or how our relationship would have naturally played out had I not tried to rush it along. And I don't want to know. Because in the five years since landing in Great Britain, I learned that I alone don't have all that much control. And that life conjures up all sorts of miraculous surprises I could never have planned nor predicted.

I could tell you that at this point, life brought me the lasting romance I had always wanted. It would have made a tidy and convenient ending to my all-consuming journey, wouldn't it?

But life is rarely that simple—at least not for me, and not in the ways I expect.

Nine years after we said goodbye, The Boyfriend used the marvels of email to track me down and told me what I thought I'd always wanted to hear:

"I've never stopped loving you."

Nine years of feasting and fasting, fasting and feasting. Is *this* what it was all supposed to come down to? I had thought of him on and off throughout the years. What's more, my mother had been having health issues, so the physical distance between us felt bigger than ever. Was I meant to move back to the US and return full circle to the only real romantic love I'd ever known?

He came to London, we reunited in a frenzy fueled by familiarity, and I followed him back to the States for a few months—until reality set in.

We were the kind of people who grow apart rather than together. At 35, I was far from the 22-year-old who had never been kissed. We argued about the same old things, except now we were also at odds about having a family. I wanted kids; he did not.

As much as we loved each other, I now knew we were only meant to be in each other's lives for a short time, and I was holding on to what I wished the relationship could have been. That doesn't mean breaking up again was easy. In many ways, it was so much harder. I had really wanted it to work, and I was wracked with guilt for leaving him again—until I remembered that he had made his choices, too.

What now?

I was angry with myself for having left London, but I also felt that I should live closer to my mother. So I stayed with her in Florida while I figured it out.

"You have to go back to London and become a British citizen," she said. "You worked so hard for it all those years."

For her, it was that simple. For me, it was the blessing I needed.

London was calling me, loudly. And maybe, despite my romantic nature, I needed to be unattached—at least for now.

I am reminded of Debbie Ford's book *The Dark Side of the Light Chasers*. In it, she writes that she spent years trying to fix herself, thinking that she would be OK when she was finally free of her weaknesses. It was an exhausting struggle. What if she gave up the fight and instead embraced what she was trying to change about herself?

What if it's OK for me to be someone who falls hard and has a hard time letting go? What if there's nothing to cure?

My pattern for getting swept up romantically goes hand in hand with the pleasure I take in food. I feel strongly. I savor deeply. These are not things I can turn on and off. They're what got me to London and what keep me writing. They're also what allow me to share my truest heart in a relationship and derive untold joy from a single ripe strawberry.

I packed my bags yet again. When I arrived at Heathrow, I was home. And I was hungry, in a different way. Returning to London was a reunion with myself and what I could create. It was the remembrance of how happy I am when I allow myself to wander, taste, and share.

I had swung from one extreme to another—from pastry training to clean eating. Now I had landed somewhere in the middle, with green smoothies at home and indulgent lunches out—sometimes by myself, often with friends.

In another unexpected development, I had found a job doing copywriting for dating and relationship experts. Now, I was getting paid to learn about love. There was much to learn.

With an entirely remote work schedule and a flat in Notting Hill, I uncovered truly good Mexican food (Taqueria), the most reliable combination of WiFi and breakfast (The Tabernacle), and what turned out to be my luckiest London find—Books for Cooks. It's a book shop with a test kitchen in the back that serves up an unbelievable deal on a three-course meal, all concocted from the thousands of books in the shop and the fresh produce from nearby Portobello Market. You eat whatever is served and sit with strangers until you become a regular and bond over how fortunate you are to have discovered the place.

I always found my people, even if I had yet to meet my guy.

I knew how to be alone, make mistakes, start over. But no woman is an island. And she always has her heart. I did know how to live from mine, with both compassion for my fellow travelers on this very human journey, and a craving—for life.

NIGHTCAP

IN LATE 2010, I moved back to the US, but London never left me, and I began writing this book—woven together out of the blog I kept while I lived abroad. Without that diary, I would never have been able to chronicle the details and emotions that sprung from all the stories you've now read. Reliving them has made me see how far I've come ... and how much has stayed the same. In October 2013, I finally met the man who would become my husband, and we honeymooned in Paris, the place I said I'd only ever return to in the company of someone I was absolutely crazy about. There, at last, was the classic fairytale finale. Except that two years later, we divorced, but not before we had our son—my true happy ending—who likes to read cookbooks at bedtime ... and teaches me what it really means to love.

ENJOY THIS BOOK?

You can make a big difference.

Reviews are a powerful tool when it comes to getting attention for books, especially books by a first-time author like me.

It has taken me years to complete *Craving London*, but it just takes a few minutes from you—in the form of an honest review—to help me find more readers. If you've enjoyed this book, I would be very grateful if you would please leave a review (it can be as short as you like) wherever you bought the book. Links to all retailers are here:

www.cravinglondonbook.com

Thank you very much.

ABOUT THE AUTHOR

Jessica Stone has spent a hearty chunk of her time plotting what to eat next and pondering the mysteries of love, both of which come together in a lot of what she writes. Her articles have appeared in *The Times, The New York Times, The Guardian, Restaurant Magazine, and Men's Health.* She lives in Pennsylvania with her son and a cat named Peppa. *Craving London* is her first book.

Connect with Jessica and **receive a bonus printable download with recipes found in *Craving London*** here:

www.jessicamstone.com/recipes

ACKNOWLEDGMENTS

I have resisted writing these acknowledgements for fear of forgetting someone, so please be gentle with me. The move to London and the completion of this book span a period of 17 years.

Reaching back in time, I'm grateful to Professor James Sutton at Florida International University for leading the study abroad program that ignited in me what became an unshakable love of the UK—including a fiery passion for Indian food.

Joanne Lawrence Gray, Deborah Norris, and Camilla Slattery provided invaluable support in helping me get set up in my adoptive city.

I made so many friends in London, only some of which appear in these pages. Each of you has been a teacher to me, and you each deserve your own volume.

There have been various drafts of this book throughout the past decade, and I am deeply grateful to all the gracious readers along the way: Victoria Jamieson, Krista Nannery, Melanie Martin Cornelius, Sara Stoneham, Arti Dwarkadas, Colleen Creighton, Linda Turner, Gayle Herring, and Rachel Danbury.

Your comments kneaded and shaped the manuscript over several much-needed rises.

On that note, I am immensely grateful to Philippa Moore who provided an exquisite critique of the earlier version, calling me out on what I needed to do most—get truly naked with the reader. You were right: it was scary but necessary.

Essential as well: my intrepid recipe testers, who provided step-by-step photos, questions, and commentary which will hopefully allow readers to re-create my food memories at home: Colleen Mullen, Linda Cardwell, Sylvia Theisen, Christine Mollica Hong, Jody Stickle Camp, Karmel Dutt, Fiona Heredia, Caroline McIntosh, Anna Velfman, Laura Di Liello, Emily Swank, Elise Walters, Audrey Brown, Jessica Havard, Kathy Rizzo, and the extraordinary teenage chef Adam Daniel (who was up for testing ALL the recipes).

Special thanks to my "big sister" Silvia Hernandez for the endless text messages of support and sage counsel. You helped me find the time to get this done. And thank you to my soul sister Andrea Warmington, for using your design talents (and patience!) to create, at once, both a satisfying and hungry cover.

Monica Stone, thank you for helping me heal both body and heart.

Marta de la Fe-Tunez, thank you for helping me put out the fires.

Cristina Garcia, thank you for the prayers.

Michelle Simmonds, thank you for coaching me through the quicksand, and from the other side of the world.

Olaf Starorypinski, you swept in as the lone brave man to test drive the manuscript. I was only slightly terrified. Thank you for bringing London to me.

Kathryn Samson, I got lucky publishing a book while you were doing the exact same thing. I look forward to talking food and film with you and Graham at a London restaurant—Italian, of course.

Jamie Roberts, I'll share dessert with you any day.

Joretta Wong, thank you for the social-media savvy, the sanity break, and the stitching.

Bill and Lorraine Diehl, my favorite showbiz couple, decade after decade: thank you for the red carpet—and "tuning in" to my stories, wherever we are.

Vanessa Kettner, from London to Easton to Paris to Skype to Whatsapp to Zoom to Facetime, I am grateful. Here's to part deux.

Kelly Higgins Bay, like the butterfly effect, your decision to publish spurred me into action. May you be wealthy in all ways.

I must thank my very patient editors, especially Daisy Olivera who went line by line, pushing me to peel layer after layer and expand on both the Cuban and British cultural norms I have come to take for granted. I'm grateful to Lorraine Broertjes for her careful copyediting, and to Kimi Farley for her proofreading prowess.

Jennifer Klear, thank you for such a positive experience vetting the manuscript. I love when life works out like that.

I am most lucky to have found mentors and role models in Gay Hendricks, Kathlyn Hendricks, and Katherine Woodward Thomas, who believed in my writing and gave me the confidence I needed to move forward. And for that, I want to thank Mary Rosenberger for entrusting me to them in the first place.

This book is dedicated to my mother, who held the vision for me long before I had it and gave me the loving wings I needed. Gracias.

Finally, thank you to all who have cheered me on and read this far.

Until we dine again.

CPSIA information can be obtained
at www.ICGtesting.com
Printed in the USA
BVHW081336050721
611158BV00018BA/747

9 781735 110202